BROKEN BODY, WOUNDED SPIRIT:
BALANCING THE SEESAW OF CHRONIC PAIN

FALL DEVOTIONS

(Revised Fall 2014)

Thank you for taking the journey with me.
In healing,
Celeste
CelesteCooper.com

Inside the Cover

"This book is a delight. From the dark world of pain and suffering comes the voice of human courage. For so many people who struggle with chronic pain, and the devoted friends who watch them and hold them, this is the map to guide them on their journey. Each page is a lamp to light the path. Keep this gentle book by your side and read it often with the one who loves you. Thank you Celeste and Jeff for your book, it is a source of strength for the soul."

> Dr John Whiteside MBBS, BSc, registered medical practitioner specializing in pain and trained by Dr Janet Travell. (Australia)

"Celeste Cooper thoughtfully shares her experience with chronic pain to help empower others to wholeheartedly live a more fulfilling and mindful life. 'Embrace what we cannot change and strive to change the things we can...' She wittingly shares healthy action strategies to help set focus on "glory days" and less on the pain. With heartfelt passion and self-awareness, Celeste and Jeff help to inspire others living with chronic pain."

> Barbara Ficarra, RN, BSN, MPA, Founder Healthin30.com, Health Educator, Award-Winning Broadcast Journalist, Featured Writer *The Huffington Post*, Sharecare Editorial Advisory Board

"Essential and inspiring — puts us in touch with our unspoken and unacknowledged inner self-understanding that gets pushed aside when pain steals our attention."

> Jan Favero Chambers, President, National Fibromyalgia and Chronic Pain Association

"The goal of living with any chronic illness is to focus on the living and move the illness to the periphery. This book beautifully collects the wisdom of the author and of the ages as daily exercises to focus on life, growth, and health despite the presence of pain. Best wishes to all who use this book to reclaim life day by day."

> Patricia Geraghty, RNC, MSN, FNP-BC, Sharecare Editorial Advisory Board

"What a wonderful book. Celeste Cooper and Jeff Miller bring inspiration and healing wisdom to those who seek relief from their symptoms or are facing illness."

> Deirdre Rawlings, PhD, ND. -- author of *Foods that Fight Fibromyalgia*, Fairwinds (2012).

"A book that does not call, it motivates one into action! It guides those with chronic pain through self-evaluation of their physical, psychological, emotional, and spiritual health, while providing education on many options available for their consideration. This will help individuals engage in their own care and personal growth. The distinctive journey each daily activity inspires readers to take is truly the icing on the cake!"

Meshea Crysup, Founder & Director fibroLIFE

BROKEN BODY, WOUNDED SPIRIT:
Balancing the SeeSaw of Chronic Pain

FALL DEVOTIONS

Celeste Cooper, RN, BSN

and

Jeff Miller, PhD

ImPress
MEDIA

Missouri

Jeff Miller and Celeste Cooper have asserted their right under the Copyright, Designs and Patents Act 1988 to be identified as the authors of this work.

Note to the reader: This book is intended as an informational guide only and not as a substitute for medical care by a qualified healthcare professional.

Edited by Cindy Leyland

Publisher Logo design by Chad Ridings
Yoga photos courtesy of Janell Ridings

All rights reserved. No part of this book may be reproduced or utilized in any form by any means, electronic or mechanical, including photocopying, recording or any information storage system without express written consent by the publisher, ImPress Media: Blue Springs, MO.

Copyright © 2013 Celeste Cooper and Jeff Miller
Revised October 2014
All rights reserved

Copyright Conventions.
ISBN-13: 978-0615638089
ISBN-10: 0615638082

Available as an EBook.

ACKNOWLEDGMENTS

This book series is dedicated to all patients who share this journey and to all of the compassionate people who are committed to helping those of us who live with daily pain. It is because of our leaders, both patients and professionals, that we are able to create a book series that will help everyone participate in the changes necessary for not only managing chronic pain, but also by transforming the way pain is perceived, judged, and treated.

We are gratified and inspired by the encouragement and support we have received for writing each of the four books. It is a privilege to provide personal and professional information to our readers, fellow advocates, and healthcare providers. We recognize all who have shared information that guides us through our own passage as writers. It is because of the wisdom Jeff and I have received from our life experiences that we understand the importance of leading a compassionate life. We would not have the ability to help others live a balanced and fulfilled life without having the gifts we have received from our families, peers, and friends.

"I am blessed to learn from my life's experiences, to grow from my mistakes, and enjoy the pleasures of accomplishment."
~Celeste

And we're off. There was a time when any notes in the margins of schoolbooks came with a penalty. I wonder now, was there an eraser posse that thumbed through every page of every textbook I ever returned?

We have created this four book series, *Broken Body, Wounded Spirit: Balancing the SeeSaw of Chronic Pain* as a tool that allows our readers to interact with the material. Feel the freedom of writing wherever you want to write, we encourage it. This book is yours to use not only as your own personal reference but also as document for your progress.

In an effort to avoid too many blank pages, maintain format, yet give extra space for notes, we have dispersed pages throughout the book for you to write your thoughts, hopes, and desires. You can locate extra NOTE pages in the index so you can fast-forward to the next NOTE page from your location. Take a moment to dog-ear the index page for your reference.

Best wishes on your journey.

Introduction

The fall season, also known as autumn, is often described as the season of gathering, preparing, ripening, and maturing. It is the time of year that represents harvest; a time of reaping the rewards of spring planting and summer growth, and it is the season of preparation for winter sustenance.

As we feast on the benefits of fall, we can relate to the aspects of self-exploration. We begin to discover mental, physical, emotional, and spiritual balance. Focusing on the maturity of the fall season prepares us for learning new strategies to help us deal with the side effects of chronic pain. Ripening of our thoughts and actions requires us to promote positive feelings and combat feelings of isolation, rejection, anxiety and the myriad of other symptoms we can experience. As we educate ourselves, we are fortified. Now is the time to arm ourselves with the tools necessary for a bountiful harvest.

Come along, it is time to begin our journey as we walk through the beautiful falling leaves that fill our path with color and diversity. Be prepared to kick up new ideas that come from this season grabbing at those of personal interest, those that entice you to learn more. Decorate your life with vast opportunities that autumn offers. Feel the crisp clean air as it fills you up and prepare for the bounty you will soon discover.

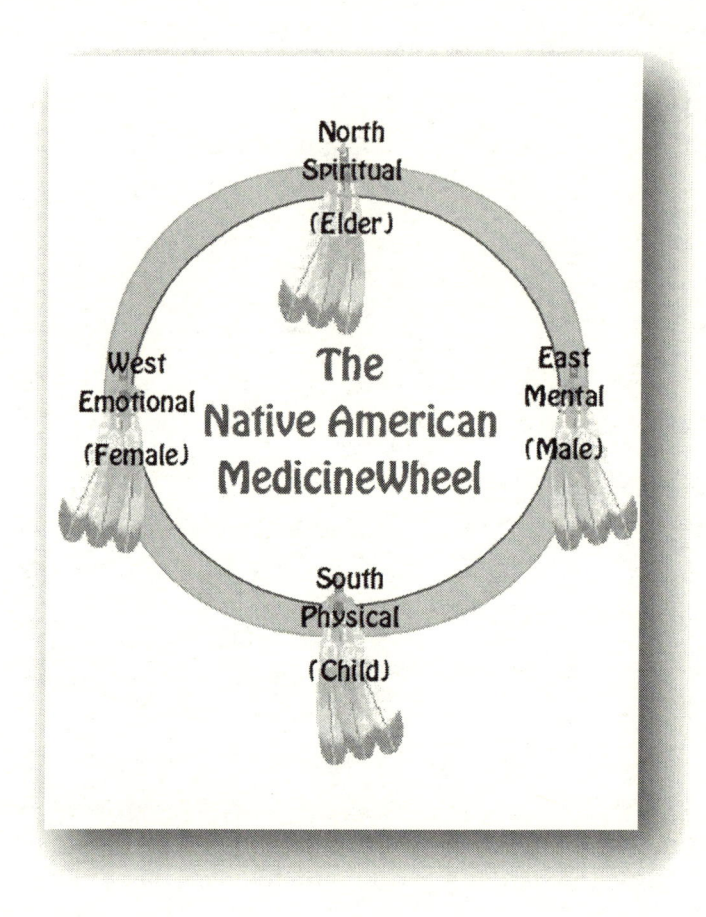

```
           North
          Spiritual
           (Elder)

West          The          East
Emotional  Native American  Mental
(Female)   MedicineWheel   (Male)

           South
          Physical
           (Child)
```

"Treating the mind, body, and spirit together gives us powerful tools for healing, each being irrevocably intertwined."

~Kathryn E. Ferner, Doctor of Psychology,
"Mind-Body-Spirit, Treating the Whole Person."
Paradigm, Spring 2003

❧ Fall ❧
Day One

The Native American Medicine Wheel

The medicine wheel has been used by Native Americans for centuries, and it is a helpful tool for teaching us about the benefits of mental, spiritual, emotional, and physical balance. Dr. Kathryn Ferner uses this philosophy in her practice, and she has written about its importance for living a full life by understanding the diversity we have within ourselves.

The "Medicine Wheel" is represented by four quadrants of a circle. The ancients laid down stones in a particular pattern with the entrance to the east facing the rising Sun. (See *Summer Devotions.*) In other books, we have equated the "Wheel" to a four-seated teeter-totter. When any one of the four seats acquires a burdensome load, it slowly starts to sink toward the ground. For instance, if our physical seat is overly burdened, the mental, emotional, and spiritual seats enter the picture. By adding more weight to one or more of the other seats, we gradually lift up the physical seat. The ability to do this brings about the balance we need to keep us equally grounded.

How can I balance my teeter-totter?

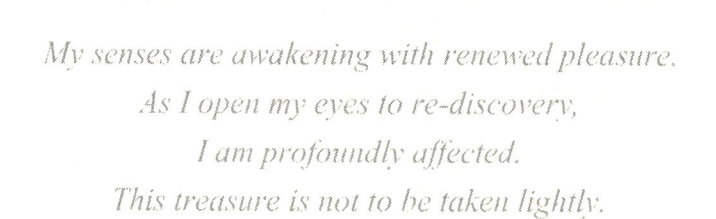

My senses are awakening with renewed pleasure.
As I open my eyes to re-discovery,
I am profoundly affected.
This treasure is not to be taken lightly.

~Celeste

Fall

Day Two

Awaken Nose, Eyes, Ears, Touch and Imagination

Describing the pleasures our senses capture can have a profound effect on how we react to our life's experiences. When we make contact with our inner being in a positive way, we create a gift, a treasure that can only be appreciated through self-exploration.

Examples:

- Feel the texture of food as it slips over your tongue.
- Explore feelings and memories attached to smelling something baking in the oven.
- Discover the senses that are awakened by watching the sunrise over the treetops.
- Focus on a bee at work as it gathers its bounty from a flower.
- Listen to an old song and recapture forgotten memories.

Enjoy the amazing way our senses can awaken from long forgotten feelings about certain life experiences.

Today I will write a short story about something that has awakened my senses.

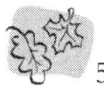

"Whatever course you decide upon, there is always
someone to tell you that you are wrong. There are always
difficulties arising, which tempt you to believe that your
critics are right. To map out a course of action
and follow it to an end requires courage."

~Ralph Waldo Emerson, 1803 – 1882

❧ Fall ❦
Day Three

Preparedness Is the Next Best Thing to an Apple Pie
Straight from the Oven on a Brisk Fall Day

Not every day presents a crisis of earth shattering magnitude. (See "Day Twenty-eight.") However, those of us who experience chronic pain do have challenges to overcome on a regular basis making it important to be aware of system breakdown predictors. Factors apparent in a total system breakdown include a loss of our physical, mental, emotional, and spiritual safety net (the four-seated teeter-totter we discuss in this series of books). If we are aware that mounting daily stressors are precursors to a crisis, can we be better prepared should a crisis occur.

Symptoms that risks are mounting:

- We become short tempered.
- We don't feel rested for several days in a row.
- We have more difficulty than usual concentrating.
- We feel overwhelmed and without resources.
- Our pain is not being managed adequately.
- We struggle with tasks that we normally manage well.

What can we do when we find a consistent pattern that could be leading up to a coping failure? We can:

- Delay chores or break them down into segments.
- Approach each day individually and break it down by each hour if necessary.
- Summon help from support system members or healthcare providers.
- Give ourselves permission to rest.
- Change what we can, and let the rest go.
- Accept that some days doing the minimum allows us to charge our battery and prevent a total breakdown later.
- Focus on our successes.

What can I add to the list of warning signs?

I will add to the list of what I can do each day to prevent a complete power failure.

Notes

*"If you know the art of breathing, you have
the strength, wisdom, and courage of ten tigers."*

~Anonymous Chinese Adage

~ Fall ~
Day Four

Is the Only CAM in Your Car?
Exploring the Compliments

CAM stands for "Complementary and Alternative Medicine." Today, many healthcare providers are embracing a "holistic" approach for patient care, because some complementary therapies have shown benefits.

Some complimentary therapies include biofeedback, myofascial therapy, chiropractic care, acupuncture, acupressure, exercise, stretching, T'ai Chi, Yoga, rocking chair therapy, and Qi Gong. Different types of bodywork might include Hellerwork, massage therapy, trigger point therapy, Alexander technique, cranio-sacral therapy, myofascial release, reflexology, Rolfing, Rosen method, spray and stretch, Trager work, and Vodder manual lymphatic drainage. They are useful for any patient living with daily chronic pain.

(Read more in *Integrative Therapies for Fibromyalgia, Chronic Fatigue Syndrome, and Myofascial Pain: The Mind-Body Connection*, and in other books in this series.)

Is there a CAM that might help me?

Finding my inner Queen
Finding my inner King

~Celeste

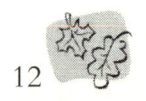

ℱall

Day Five

Pondering My Uniqueness

Who am I without pain?
(*Fill in the blanks.*)

_____

_____

_____

Now answer these questions:

What outings can I plan when I'm able?
How can I be funny?
Am I a pleasure to be around?
Do I find joy?
How can I consider others?

_____

_____

_____

*I am grateful for every human being who
has taught me the value of determination
and for those who join me in the process.*

~Celeste

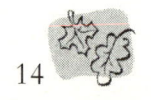

Fall

Day Six

Willpower and Resolve

If we have the willpower to create something positive, we will. Put wisely by Maya Angelou:

> "You can only become truly accomplished at something you love. Don't make money your goal. Instead, pursue the things you love doing and then do them so well that people can't take their eyes off of you."

We are equipped to meet the challenges pain can bring because we all have an innate desire to do what we love. We are drawn to people who love what they do and intuitively want what they have. This is human.

When we approach inner conflict with willpower and resolve, when we replace conflict with pursuit, we begin to change.

I will begin each day anew with willpower and resolve to accomplish something I love.

"To be free from evil thoughts is God's best gift."

~ Aeschylus, Poet, 525- 456 BC

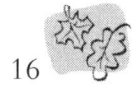

ॐ Fall ॐ
Day Seven

The Tree of Life Grows
Nourishing It with Affirmations

When we think in an affirmative manner about ourselves, our body, our place in this world, and our purpose, we begin to treat ourselves with thoughts and feelings of concern and comfort. We should care for ourselves as we would any friend in physical, emotional, mental, or spiritual pain. We wouldn't judge them by harsh standards, nor should we judge ourselves in that way. Writing affirmations and living an affirmative life puts an end to a destructive inner dialogue. (See *Summer Devotions* for more information.)

As you move through this book, you will note affirmations or inspiring quotes on the opposite page. Use them as a guide. A few hints for writing affirmations are:

- Keep them relevant.
- Keep them positive.
- Keep them simple.
- Commit yourself.

Today I will plant my own tree of loving forgiveness.

FALL DEVOTIONS, authors Cooper & Miller

"The past is our definition. We may strive, with good reason, to escape it, or to escape what is bad in it, but we will escape it only by adding something better to it."

~Wendell Berry, American academic,
and author of *New Collected Poems*, *The Unsettling of America*,
and more...

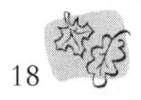

Fall
Day Eight

To Get up, We Must First Fall Down
Learning from Our Experiences

If we look for the lesson, we soon learn to use our mistakes as motivation for accomplishment. Until we acknowledge them, however, we can't learn from them in a meaningful way. Mistakes we can learn from include:

- Neglect of self-awareness.
- Developing a defensive behavior.
- Using unhealthy strategies for coping with pain.
- Arguing.
- Expecting that others should feel our pain.
- Setting unreasonable goals.
- Holding ourselves to an irrational standard.
- Disregard for self-management.
- Mismanagement of perpetuating factors.
- Isolating ourselves from others.
- Disregard for appreciation.

> "A life spent making mistakes is not only more honorable, but more useful than a life spent doing nothing."
>
> ~George Bernard Shaw

What mistakes can I learn from to lead a balanced life?

"At the touch of love, everyone becomes a poet."

Plato, 429–347 BC

Fall

Day Nine

Love in Poetry

Some poetry can only be interpreted by the author, others, by the reader with his or her own ideas on what the poem says. There is no need to think you can't write your own poem. Here are a few tips.

- It doesn't have to rhyme.
- Pick some favorite words from the dictionary, a book on flowers or birds, or even the telephone directory.
- Add shapes, sounds, texture, color, or smells.
- Put your own spin on it, and let your mind run wild.
- Remember your poetry can be on a real or imaginary experience.
- Title your poem before or after you write it, because there are no boundaries.
- There is no specific length. It can be one sentence.

Poetry has been defined as a gateway to self-exploration and awareness. Have fun, enjoy.

(See "Day Twenty-seven," and "Day Seventy-five.")

Today I will start a poem.

*Mindful awareness expands my being and encourages
me to live consciously, without judgment.*

~Celeste

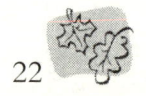

❦ Fall ❧

Day Ten

Being Mindful of Our Thoughts and Body

If we cultivate mindfulness in our life, we see everything has value. (See "Mindfulness through Meditation and Prayer" in *Spring Devotions*.) Dr. Jon Kabat-Zinn, Professor of Medicine Emeritus and creator of the Stress Reduction Clinic at the University of Maryland Medical Center is the author of *Full Catastrophic Living: Using the Wisdom of Your Body and Mind to Face Stress, Pain and Illness*, and numerous other books to ease suffering by reducing stress and pain through meditation. He tells us we may not always like the sensations we are experiencing from pain, but by acknowledging our pain without judgment, we bring ourselves to a higher level of self-awareness. Neuroscience tells us we can effect physiologic changes in our body by using the teachings of Dr. Kabat-Zinn and others.

Think of a bright fall day, briskness on the edge of arriving, leaves a colorful artist's pallet, and migrant birds flying overhead in the backdrop of a crisp blue sky. These are examples of being mindful. All we have to do is be present and aware in the moment admonishing our role as critic.

How is being mindful important to me today?

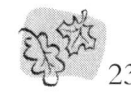

*I'm not a shipwreck.
I am the vessel that sets sail on a course of healing,
without pain, maybe not, but healing nonetheless.*

~Celeste

Fall
Day Eleven

Terms in the Company of Pain
Chiropractic Medicine

Chiropractic medicine is a healthcare system that focuses on maintaining the health of the nervous system by therapeutic manipulation of the skeletal bones and joints to align the spine and soft tissues in order to facilitate delivery of nerve impulses and the flow of vital energy.

A good chiropractor understands and treats muscles, their coverings and extensions, tendons, and ligaments, which are connective tissue in the body. Connective tissue disruption is often involved in pain disorders and disrupts the nature flow of cellular energy important to healing. Chiropractors understand how dysfunction of any of these things can be an aggravation to pain, and their treatment plan's goal is to restore the body's alignment so the body functions as it should.

Finding a chiropractor that specializes in soft tissue as well as spinal restoration is important. Referrals by someone with similar conditions are always best.

*Conversation is in the absence of silence,
yet, stillness speaks volumes.*

~Celeste

Fall
Day Twelve

Speech Is Not All Verbal

internal dialogue = a dialogue with our innermost self, described as self-talk. Internal dialogue is what you say non-verbally to yourself, about yourself, about something else, or about someone else.

external communication = a verbal or written exchange of information with another, such as conversation, letters or email.

body language = non-verbal clues by body positioning and expression, smile vs. grimace, withdrawal vs. reaching out, laughing vs. crying, guarding vs. no response, etc.

(You can get tips for effective communication on "Day Twenty-three" and "Day Forty-six," and the "Doctor Patient Relationship" in *Spring Devotions.*)

*"If I had to live my life again,
I'd make the same mistakes, only sooner."*

~Tallulah Bankhead, actress, 1903 - 1968

❦ Fall ❧

Day Thirteen

On Pointe

Learning from our mistakes has long been admired as strength of character. As people in chronic pain, we may fall prey to unhealthy ways of coping. In an effort to learn from those mistakes, we should focus on healthy mechanisms, such as clearing out the cerebral trash that clutters our thinking.

Healthy action strategies might include:

- Taking advantage of diversion opportunities.
- Fortifying healthy relationships.
- Taking a walk.
- Doing for someone else.
- Joining a support group.
- Getting outdoors.
- Setting achievable goals.

When we do this, we make way for new and better ways of dealing with the side effects of chronic pain and illness.

What healthy coping strategies can I use to get my life "On Pointe?"

Notes

Notes

*Expectations are goals that don't have to
necessarily be met; it's really more about
the perception of our passage.*

~Celeste

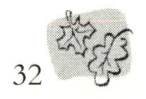

ॐ Fall ॐ
Day Fourteen

Being Flexible Is More than Touching Our Toes

Adapting to change isn't always easy, especially if we don't learn to embrace it as an opportunity. Having chronic pain creates change, and like it or not, we must learn that physical alterations also affect us mentally, emotionally, and spiritually.

There are times when we are harder on ourselves than we need to be. We should acknowledge what we cannot change and strive to change the things we can, such as learning new hobbies, modifying chores to meet our needs, forming or fortifying relationships that help us be our best, or changing doctors when we don't feel our needs are being met in a prudent manner.

There is a great little storybook written about change called, *"Who Moved My Cheese?"* by Spencer Johnson, MD. *We have no financial or other connections with this book. It's a short read and very insightful.

How can I be more "flexible" with myself today?

*My being is sketched from strength and weakness;
I aspire to inspire others in this exercise of self-awareness.*

~Celeste

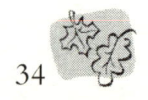

❧ Fall ☙

Day Fifteen

Revelations

The Big Reveal

Revelations are those things that open our eyes, hearts, and minds. Here is an exercise that will open you up to full discovery and expose you to a new way of seeing yourself.

We all have strengths and weaknesses so no judgment is necessary. This is merely an exercise of becoming better acquainted with who you are and what you have to share.

My Strengths   My Weaknesses

"Who of you by worrying can add
a single hour to his life?"
Mathew 6:27, NIV

*When I find my calm,
I discover refuge for myself.*

~Celeste

❧ Fall ❦
Day Sixteen

Anxiety

Have you experienced the feeling of only having one nerve left and someone is sitting on IT? Having chronic pain gives us a variety of reasons to feel anxious. We experience mental, emotional, social, and physical stress. Sometimes, we experience financial difficulties in relationship to living with pain, and that has a trickledown effect. Anxiety raises our heart rate and blood pressure, causes sleep disturbance, and wreaks havoc on our well-being. Anxiety can be the root of anger, agitation, fear, or depression, and it is very unhealthy.

Here are a few tips for dealing with "side effects" of pain:

- Don't sweat "what ifs."
- Recognize worry as a warning sign.
- Have a crisis plan. *(See* "Day Three" and "Day Twenty-eight.")
- Identify and avoid triggers.
- Try biofeedback. (See "Day Seventy-two.")
- Practice meditation regularly. (See *Winter* and *Spring Devotions.)*

What are my stressors and how can I avoid them?

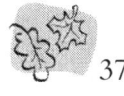

*Forward motion is a choice,
chance the opportunity to generate momentum.*

~Celeste

❦ *Fall* ❦

Day Seventeen

Managing Your Opportunities

Opportunity provides an opening, a prospect, an option to break through the dungeon of negative energy.

Putting opportunities into action:

- Watch the sunset.
- Help a friend.
- Help a co-worker.
- Lend an ear.
- Hug your loved one.
- Laugh with a child.
- Listen to stories told by an elder.
- Tell somebody what you like about him or her.
- Write a poem.
- Share a happy event.
- Smile at a stranger.
- When standing in a line or stuck in traffic, let someone in front of you.

We become aware of the opportunities that surround us when we make them the focus of getting through the day.

What are my opportunities?

FALL DEVOTIONS, authors Cooper & Miller

"Know what's weird? Day by day, nothing
seems to change. But pretty soon,
everything is different."

~Calvin & Hobbes, a syndicated daily comic strip
written and illustrated by
American cartoonist Bill Watterson

❧ Fall ❧
Day Eighteen

Periodic Review
Over the Past Six Months

Name   Date

Treatments have provided:

No relief   Complete Relief
0%   20%   40%   60%   80%   100%

Medications have provided:

No relief   Complete Relief
0%   20%   40%   60%   80%   100%

New coping strategies have provided:

No relief   Complete Relief
0%   20%   40%   60%   80%   100%

I will circle the percentage as it applies and share it with my healthcare providers.

A packed life is crowded with tasks;
a full life is balanced with appreciating opportunities,
fellowship with others, and the love of humankind.

~Celeste

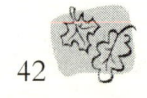

Fall

Day Nineteen

Defining Triggers, Conquering Control

Inappropriate management of aggravating factors to your pain and/or fatigue can trigger many symptoms.

Aggravating factors might include:

- Poor posture.
- Nutritional deficiencies.
- Poor sleep habits.
- Lack of acceptance (Sometimes, doing everything right isn't enough—have an action plan.)
- Weather changes. (You can't change it, but you can minimize other annoying factors.)
- Poor control of coexisting conditions.
- Poor coping mechanisms.
- Neglect of spiritual and/or emotional needs.
- Medications.
- Tight clothing or shoes.
- Symptom neglect.

My triggers are...

*Looking back ten years, knowing how I feel today,
I appreciate the now, because in ten years, I will look
back and remember these days as the good days.*

~Celeste

🍂 Fall 🍂

Day Twenty

Challenging Your Brain Power

Chronic pain interferes with sleep; lack of sleep interferes with thinking straight; and some disorders cause brainfog. Here are some tips for saving cognitive function:

- Give yourself plenty of time.
- Solicit help from friends and family when in crisis.
- Practice the suggestions on organizing you found in this book.
- Write things down in the same place every time.
- Assess how much is too much.
- Assess how much is not enough.
- Focus on mental balance.
- Weigh priorities of your mental in-box.
- Read a good book to provide your brain with witty calisthenics.

When we take a few minutes to make these assessments, we are in a better position when we are challenged. (See "Day Thirty-nine.")

I will put this on my refrigerator.

FALL DEVOTIONS, authors Cooper & Miller

"Many of life's failures are people who did not
realize how close they were to success
when they gave up."

~Thomas A. Edison, 1847 – 1931

Fall

Day Twenty-one

Take a Stand

People who survive chronic pain make the best advocates and advocacy is a good way to vent frustrations in a healthy and meaningful way. Those of us in chronic pain have felt discriminated against at some time or another. If you haven't, you will. Try to turn that anger into something positive. Not only will you avoid internalizing it, you will experience the cathartic effect of letting go.

September, a fall month, is Pain Awareness Month. Join an organization that promotes pain awareness. Find others with common goals, and support those who support us. Spread the word, you will raise awareness by speaking from your heart. Write letters to important people, even if you don't think they will read them.

Tips for writing an advocacy letter:

- First Gear: "The hook" – A statement that will engage the reader
- Second Gear: "Personalize it"
- Third Gear: "State your case"
- Forth Gear: Full Speed Ahead—"Ask for follow up and be prepared to respond"

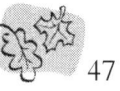

- Attachments: [Name any attachments that support your letter and its content.]
- Copy: [List anyone you feel would benefit from knowing you have sent out your letter.]

Ten top tips for advocacy:

1. Pick a topic that riles you up.
2. Share.
3. Respect your limits.
4. Set achievable goals.
5. Accept your right to be heard.
6. Accept that you might not always get a reply or the reply you want, but believe that somebody is listening. We never know how far or how wide we are received.
7. Stay organized.
8. Carry your advocacy into your own healthcare.
9. Provide a mechanism for follow up.
10. Remember you are on a team.

Excerpt from Celeste's website "Elements of Advocacy" at http://TheseThree.com

How can I make a difference?

Notes

"Consult not your fears but your hopes and your dreams. Think not about your frustrations, but about your unfulfilled potential. Concern yourself not with what you tried and failed in, but with what is still possible for you to do."

~Pope John XXIII, 1881-1963

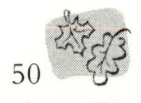

❧ Fall ❧

Day Twenty-two

Tasks Are More Manageable in Small Increments

Tips for breaking tasks down so you can better manage them:

- Don't try to do too much at one time.
- Expect that if you overdo today, you will be spent for tomorrow.

Fall is reserved for preparing for winter:

- Rather than cleaning out all the cabinets at once, plan to do one cabinet per day.
- Pack away clothes and bring out winter apparel one closet a day.
- Clean up leaves or do fall outdoor cleanup one section of the yard at a time.

Get up and fix something right now. Change a light bulb, tighten a screw, clean out a vegetable bin, and throw away your old socks—Feel better? Five minutes, tops, you'll sleep better, too.

What did I do?

How can I break down tasks so they are better managed?

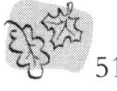

"Happiness is a sunbeam which may pass through a thousand bosoms without losing a particle of its original ray; nay, when it strikes on a kindred heart, like the converged light on a mirror, it reflects itself with redoubled brightness. It is not perfected 'til it is shared."

~Jane Porter, author of *The Good Wife*, *The Good Daughter*, and more...

🍂 Fall 🍂

Day Twenty-three

Putting Stuff out to Pasture

Chronic pain and illness can damage our relationships with others and with ourselves, but we can effect a positive change in our lives. We can learn to love again and put the side effects of chronic illness to pasture grazing alongside the other negative aspects of pain. They might want to come into the barn from time to time, but we're not cattle; we aren't stuck in one space of grazing or thinking.

Anger accompanied by hostility and resentment may be necessary evils of working through the grieving process, but when we don't move forward in that process, these attitudes can fester like an untreated infection and damage our relationships. So when we get past that stage, it is time to think about how we can nurture our love and commitment, not only for others, but ourselves too. If we put an equal amount of effort into loving as we do into coping with pain, we just might find that dealing with pain's many aspects gets easier.

I will put anger out to pasture and welcome love and commitment.

"*Your pain is the breaking of the shell that enclos101es your understanding.*"

~Khalil Gibran

Fall

Day Twenty-four

Terms in the Company of Pain
The "P" in Pain

pain = a feeling of distress, suffering, or agony caused by stimulation to specific nerve endings.

acute pain = pain that alerts the sufferer to early tissue damage somewhere in the body; it is a protective mechanism.

chronic pain = pain that has outlived its usefulness as a warning signal that something is wrong.

pain threshold = the level that must be reached for a stimulus to be recognized as painful.

paresthesia = abnormal sensation numbness, burning or prickling.

peripheral pain = pain that is experienced from input from muscles, organs, joints, or anywhere outside the central nervous system.

"It may be alright to be content with what you have, never with what you are."

~ Anonymous

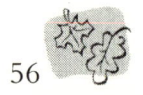

❧ Fall ❧
Day Twenty-five

Coming Front and Center

Is your greatest need:

- Physical?
- Mental?
- Emotional?
- Spiritual?

Tips for satisfying your needs:

- Read a self-help book.
- Write a prayer. (See *Winter* and *Spring Devotions.*)
- Address aggravating factors of your pain. (See *Summer Devotions.*)
- Identify alleviating factors of your pain.
- Listen to soothing music, such as nature sounds.
- Meditate.
- Rest.
- Stretch.
- Call a friend.
- Write a positive dialogue with your body.

How can I meet my needs today?

A broken body needs a good body shop.

~Celeste

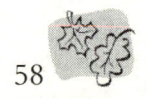

🌿 Fall 🌿
Day Twenty-six

Work That Body, Trim Those Sails

A good body worker will help you keep moving with the least amount of stress to your body. Finding the right therapist is as important as finding the right doctor.

A qualified massage therapist should:

- Be licensed to practice in his/her state. (Most states require specific standards of performance for massage therapists.)

- Be certified by the National Certification Board for Therapeutic Massage and Bodywork.
  http://www.ncbtmb.org/

- Be a graduate or student of a school accredited by the Commission on Massage Therapy Accreditation.
  http://www.comta.org/

A recommendation by a family member, friend, or colleague is often your best resource.

> Different types of bodywork are discussed in *Spring Devotions* and *Summer Devotions*.

Should I consider massage to trim my sails?

I don't have to be a poet to express myself freely through poetry.

~Celeste

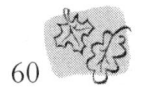

❧ Fall ❧

Day Twenty-seven

My Bridge by Celeste Cooper

Abandoned old bridge, listen, there's music below,
Birds sing, bushes rustle, dancing lights give a show.
Roaring rapids keep time within my stone's throw,
Columbine speak, pine trees gaze, and the aspens glow.

A chorus of flora, fauna on the edge of waters flow.
Oh what a sight—my bridge to bestow.

A watershed sanctuary has mercy, it doesn't annoy.
Bridge pleading, "Protect my story" do not destroy.
Worn bridge of immigrants, imaginations employ,
Weathered, tattered, once the route of a convoy.

Bridge of history, share the story of what you enjoy,
Oh what a sight, my bridge, I do enjoy.

Pattering feet, wagon wheels, laughter in mind,
Days gone, aware this bridge, a world joined to mine.
Oh what a sight my bridge—this is divine.

What or who touched my heart enough to write a poem?

"Moderate or severe persisting pain of long duration that disrupts sleep and normal living, ceases to serve a protective function and instead degrades health and functional capacity."

~Chapman and Stillman, authors of
Pathological Pain, Handbook of Perception: Pain and Touch.
Edited by Krueger L. New York, Academic Press, 1996

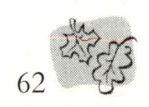

❧ Fall ❧

Day Twenty-eight

Moderating Pain and Function When in Crisis

Crisis management is practiced by many. For instance, it's important that firefighters know what to do when the alarm sounds, that schoolchildren know how to execute a fire drill, that utility personnel know what to do in the case of a power failure, or a company know what to do in the case of a computer hacking.

In every one of these instances, there is a course of action called "The Crisis Management Plan," and every time the crisis plan has to be executed, we learn. Those that plan for disasters do a reassessment after a plan is executed. They ask questions like, "How did the plan work?—"Did anything happen that we weren't prepared for?"—"Can we improve on the plan so it doesn't happen again?" This is why we should have a plan in case of a flare of symptoms.

We can do some things to be prepared, such as:

- Manage our time appropriately.
- Recognize and respect our limitations.
- Avoid setting unrealistic goals.

- Learn from the experience and be prepared to make changes to the plan.
- Expect the unexpected.

Things we should remember when we are in a crisis:

- We are on a team; we should solicit help where we can.
- Employ successful treatment strategies.
- Have a crisis partner, someone we can talk to when an emergency arises.
- Remember, some things take time.
- Accept that sometimes, even though we do our best, it doesn't affect the outcome.
- We must deal with the crisis until it passes.

Draw up your own crisis plan. Use the tools you are given in this book series.

My crisis plan includes:

_____

_____

_____

_____

Notes

*Bestowed on me is strength from those who
exemplify possibilities, believing in the right thing,
putting a megaphone to their voice,
acting on their words.*

~Celeste

Fall
Day Twenty-nine

At the Root of All Advocacy Is the Activist

As discussed on ""Day Twenty-one," there is another way of using anger and fear. We can exploit it by using our voice for change.

Here are some additional tips for becoming a change agent:

- Support lobbyist activities in Congress and the National Institute of Health.
- Write your senators and legislators.
- Become familiar with the pain laws of your state.
- Write letters to healthcare organizations.
- Write letters to the insurance commissioners.
- Form a petition and send it to your local representatives.
- Support an advocacy organization.
- Share information within your support network.
- Join an online group that promotes advocacy projects.

I cannot tell you the number of times I have found great personal support through my advocacy networks.

(See *Winter Devotions* for more information on advocacy.)

How can I use my voice?

"Friends are those rare people who ask how we are and then wait to hear the answer."

~Ed Cunningham, former professional American football player and football analyst for CBS and ABC

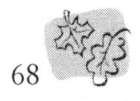

Fall

Day Thirty

Relationship Roulette

Energy is a limited commodity to those of us in chronic pain. It should be valued and expended on relationships that will promote a sense of security and trust. Expect that the other person wants to share with you and expects you to share with them in return. This type of relationship is one we should nurture and protect.

A relationship that puts us on the defensive doesn't encourage us to be our best nor does it provide mutual respect. Instead, an unhealthy relationship drains us of precious energy. It could be in our best interest to avoid relationship roulette.

What relationship should I nurture? _____

Why? _____

If any, what relationship should I let go? _____

Why? _____

"If we could see the miracle of a single flower clearly, our whole life would change."

~Buddha

❧ Fall ❧

Day Thirty-one

SPIRITUALITY

The Fourth Seat on Our Four Seated Teeter Totter

Pain has the ability to affect every part of us, making perpetual enrichment of our spirit vital to balance and feelings of well-being. Spirituality is a very personal experience, and being spiritual is not the same as being religious, or vice versa.

According to Roger Walsh, MD, PhD, In *The 7 Central Practices to Awaken Heart and Mind: Essential Spirituality*, there are seven practices common to all great religions.

1. Reduce cravings and greed.
2. Cultivate emotional wisdom, love, and gratitude.
3. Live an ethical life by feeling and doing well.
4. Develop a peaceful mind, and strive to reach calm.
5. Awaken awareness of all things sacred.
6. Cultivate spiritual awareness.
7. Embrace the generosity and joy of service.

You can find more information on spirituality throughout this book series.

What spiritual practices can I use to foster spiritual growth?

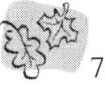

FALL DEVOTIONS, authors Cooper & Miller

Being mindful of my senses, taste, feel, sight and hearing, reminds me of the miracles in my life.

~Celeste

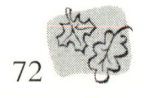

❧ Fall ❧

Day Thirty-two

Notions and Potions

Think of your favorite drink. Now, define why you chose it. Is it because it quenches your thirst at the end of a difficult day? On the other hand, is there a potion you enjoy with a friend? Is it that first cup of coffee or juice that starts your day? Is it a good cup of hot chocolate topped with luscious, fluffy, whipped cream as you sit by the hearth while the fall season prepares for winter?

Next time you enjoy your favorite drink, keep these notions in mind. Feel the potion as it touches your lips, examine the texture, and taste as it glides down your throat. Why is it familiar to you? Does it bring back any special memories? Does it tingle as it makes its journey? Does it warm your spirit? Does it remind you of a hot summer's day or a chilly fall afternoon by the fire?

Am I drinking mindfully? If not, what can I change?

Which is best, the notion or the potion? Could it be both?

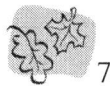

*"The measure of choosing well is whether a man likes
and finds good in what he has chosen."*

~Charles Lamb, alias Elia, 1775–1834,
English essayist and critic

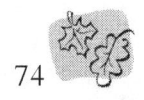

Fall

Day Thirty-three

Empowerment

How do you feel when a friend, or even a stranger, asks for your help? Are you annoyed, angered, or do you feel put upon? Do you despise the other person as weak or incompetent? Of course you don't! (If you answered yes, see a therapist immediately.)

> (Excerpt from Integrative Therapies for Fibromyalgia, Chronic Fatigue Syndrome, and Myofascial Pain: The Mind-Body Connection by Celeste Cooper, RN and Jeff Miller, PhD)

Disaster after disaster shows us that we treasure the opportunity to be of service. We aspire to be part of a solution, and we cherish that "thank you" more than any other words of that day. Why would you deny another person this kind of satisfaction? Helping others is gratifying and empowering. Next time you really need help remember this.

How do I define empowerment?

When I really need help, will I ask for it?

How can I help others?

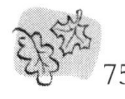

*Seeds of kindness sown in fertile soil
replenish the earth with love.*

~Celeste

Fall

Day Thirty-four

Kindness

"Do not keep the alabaster box of your friendship sealed up until your friends are dead. Fill their lives with sweetness. Speak approving, cheering words while their ears can hear them, and while their hearts can be thrilled and made happier. The kind of things you mean to say when they are gone, say before they go."

~ George William Childs,
publisher and philanthropist, 1829-1894

Where, how, or to whom shall I plant my seeds of kindness?

*I strive to live each moment with peace, clarity, resolution,
and appreciation, because it is possible,
and it is all that I have.*

~Celeste

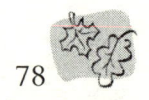

❧ Fall ✥

Day Thirty-five

Journaling for Gold

When in physical pain, it is important to nurture our mental, emotional, and spiritual aspects of being. When we become lopsided, journaling is an effective way to upright our leaning ship. It provides the sail that keeps our vessel sea worthy. Journaling helps us:

- Identify behaviors that block awareness and growth.
- Guide wellness.
- Explore awareness of self and others.
- Set and achieve life goals.
- Promote problem solving.
- Develop spontaneity and positive attitude.
- Pinpoint and address stressors.
- Communicate effectively with self.
- Work through feelings safely.
- Explore dreams.

(See "Day Forty-two" the *Winter Devotions* of this series.)

What three things can I journal about today?

1) _____

2) _____

3) _____

"Keep your eyes on the stars
and your feet on the ground."

~Theodore Roosevelt

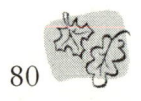

ॐ Fall ॐ
Day Thirty-six

Terms in the Company of Pain
Chronic Pain

Pain is caused by stimulation of nerves that signal the brain via chemicals called neurotransmitters. From the periphery, communication begins when neurotransmitters make their way from the injured area to the brain via the nerves, nerve roots, and spinal cord. Once they arrive at their destination, they tell the brain it needs to get to work. In ordinary circumstances, the brain will signal the fight or flight response, and red flags go up in an effort to draw attention to the area that is having difficulty functioning normally. This is what is supposed to happen. Pain is supposed to be a warning sign, and it is not supposed to live on after the initial threat has been resolved, but we know it does.

Think of neurotransmitters (discussed on Day *Forty-five* and *Day Sixty*) as postal carriers. In chronic pain, either the carrier hits a detour or the brain is bombarded with too many messages making it difficult to sort through the important information it receives in these letters. It is also possible that the brain dispatches a response, but the letter doesn't have enough postage to get it where it needs to go.

Anyone who has ever had his or her mail forwarded understands how things like this can happen. It is this breakdown of communication in chronic pain, different from what happens in acute pain, which leads experts to believe that chronic pain is a disease in and of itself.

How our brain deals with pain not only has a physiological response. When we cut our skin or break a bone, we often avoid looking at the injury. We begin a dialogue of "it hurts, but if I look, it could be worse." I know this is what my son reported when he experienced a compound fracture of both of the bones in his forearm. He described the experience as unreal. Possibly, it is the mind's protective mechanism to prepare us for the emotional shock of it all.

As much as we know about neuroscience, we know we don't know everything. It is impossible to define how the mind works even though we understand more about the brain as an organ. Therefore, those of us with chronic pain should be aware of how changes in our perception could have an effect not only on how we cope, but also on how our brain is trained to respond from previous emotional reactions. Emergency responders will tell you people in acute pain who do not catastrophize their injury or illness generally do better at coping with their injury.

How do my experiences affect the way I respond to pain?

Notes

"Karma is to become fully alive through honoring the uniqueness of one's incarnation."

~Baba Ram Dass, Richard Alpert,
Western born yogi and spiritual teacher,
and motivational speaker

❧ Fall ❧

Day Thirty-seven

Karma

Many of us have said things like "Karma can be a bitch," suggesting that if we do something unkind, the thought, word, or deed will eventually come back to us. The Christian bible says, "As ye reap, so shall ye sow." If we do something kind, we will be rewarded. However, should we consider "Karma" as cause and effect?

Karma is an Indian religious concept of action or deed. It is an intangible thing, like faith. As human beings, we have consciousness that links us to our spirituality. We store past events, feelings, and reactions that will one day be born again as our Karma, good or bad, and without judgment.

Buddhists believe Karma is the outcome of our own past and present actions. The good in us seeks enlightenment, clarity, and vision to carry positive energy into the world. Without Karma, we could not become enlightened; without enlightenment, we would be void of positive potential. Without errors and acts of humanity, we would not have experiences that make us a better person.

How am I unique in this respect?

"A healthy diet is the cornerstone of
a healthy lifestyle."

~ Andrew Weil, MD,
author, integrative health, and wellness expert

Fall

Day Thirty-eight

Challenge Yourself!

Nutrition plays a huge role in our health, including pain. Preservatives and mass production of food to fulfill our needs as a society have created a health crisis.

If we think of food as energy for our cells that make up our body, it only makes sense that "we are what we eat." We are seeing an upsurge in autoimmune diseases, and the effects of our diet on the gut are believed to play a significant role.

We should challenge ourselves to eat fresh foods, minimize processed foods, and limit junk food to an occasional treat. Then, we can see how we feel.

Begin to keep track of what you eat. Buy a calendar at a dollar store and write down what you consume each day. If you have a flare of symptoms or experience a new symptom, look back at your calendar to see if you can identify any trends regarding what you are consuming.

What nutritional changes can I make for a healthier lifestyle?

*My life's goals are satisfied
because of my willingness to accept
the change of my circumstances.*

~Celeste

Fall

Day Thirty-nine

Clearing the Fog

When brainfog takes over, it is easy to become overwhelmed and allow negative internal dialogue to intervene. There are ways of preparing for, and dealing with, brainfog.

We should:

- Employ tactics that have helped in the past.
- Try not to make life-altering decisions when in fog.
- Bring pain under control.
- Keep to a routine.
- Postpone activities that lead to fatigue.
- Examine other disorders that might lead to fog, such as metabolic problems.
- Evaluate the side effects of our medication.
- Accept that in the case of some diseases, brainfog is out of our control.
- Be kind to ourselves and ignore the comments of those who are in the wake of our fog unless they are providing important feedback.

These tips should keep us from self-judgment.

What intellectual goals have I met that affect how I deal with my needs?

*Quiet time offers self-reflection,
mindfulness, and spiritual rejuvenation.*

~Celeste

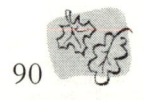

Fall

Day Forty

We Are a Package, the Whole Package

The next time you are near a bookstore or newsstand, invest some money in a magazine, or two, that covers one of your hobbies or interests, not a work-related magazine or newspaper. Pick up one that is informational about something you like, such as cooking, surfing, computers, kids, or a hobby you would like to try. Put the magazines under the passenger seat of your car or in a briefcase, purse, or backpack. The next time you are pushed into "wait" mode by circumstances, start reading.

Think of this as an exercise for taking out the mental trash. Before you know it, you may look forward to having to wait. You may even show up early for your appointments so you can pass the time reading about something you enjoy.

How can I change waiting into an opportunity?

FALL DEVOTIONS, authors Cooper & Miller

"A cheerful heart is good medicine,
but a downcast spirit dries up the bones."

~Proverbs 17:22

❧ *Fall* ❧

Day Forty-one

Terms in the Company of Pain
Allopathic Medicine

According to www.thenewmedicine.org, "Allopathy is the type of medicine most familiar to westerners today. Allopathy is a biologically based approach to healing. For instance, if a patient has high blood pressure, an allopathic physician might give him/her a drug that lowers blood pressure." (See *Fall Devotions*, "Allopathic vs. Naturopathic.")

"In 1848, the allopathic rationalists create the American Medical Association (AMA) and gain a strong organizational edge. Even though many American clinics once relied on homeopathy and naturopathy, allopathic medicine quickly rises to dominance. Allopathy's popularity is due to successful scientific progress including the production of certain vaccines and development of specific drugs that treat disease." It is a method of treating disease with remedies that produce effects different from those caused by the disease itself. Your MD or DO is an allopathic doctor.

Allopathic medicine is important in treating chronic pain, but there is evidence to suggest that we do better when we incorporate complementary medicine. *(See "Day Four.")*

"No man is a failure who enjoys life."

~William Feather, 1889 – 1981,
American publisher and author

❧ Fall ❧

Day Forty-two

Word Energy – Event Journaling

Event journaling has a different twist. It requires us to write about things we enjoy doing or things we imagine would be fun. You can easily find topics to write about by making a word list and moving on from there.

I Like:

- vacations
- camping
- taking pictures
- talking
- friends
- meditation
- nature
- the sunset
- .....
- ......

(See more on journaling on "Day Thirty-five" and in *Winter Devotions* of this series.)

What event is so special to me that I want to write about it?

*I strive to see potential
where others see impossibilities.*

~Celeste

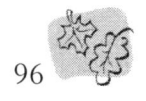

Fall

Day Forty-three

Terms in the Company of Pain
Neuralgia

Neuralgia is pain caused by a disturbance of normal nerve function. It can cause extreme pain. While there are some alternatives for treatment, there is room for improvement.

Following is an exercise that you can do any time. It doesn't require a doctor's order, and it can't make you worse.

> Imagine your nerves, each one a different color representing a different part of the body; they are all tangled up in a bundle, like a ball of yarn a cat has played with. Now imagine that ball floating in a pool of soothing, thick, warm liquid. As the ball starts to relax, it untangles and each nerve starts to leisurely unwrap until they are all resting on top of the pool. Now, imagine each one being soothed and mended. As you do this, move your focus to your breathing. Each breath should be relaxed and the tension present in your chest, shoulders, neck, and the rest of your body should feel like jelly.

Do this exercise as often as you need until all the restrictions are gone.

I will do this exercise when I feel like a bundle of nerves.

*May our spirit fill us with
understanding of victory and defeat,
and the necessity of falling down
so we can find our way up.*

~Celeste

98

🍂 Fall 🍂

Day Forty-four

Setting Goals

Goals are those things we keep our eye on, they are the things we plan to do. Goals and plans help us measure progress in our lives, but care should be given to set goals that are achievable. The goal may remain the same, but prepare for adjustments in your plan. We are all a work in progress.

Every plan includes, what, when, why and how.

- Define **what** you want.
- **When** do you plan to complete your goal?
- **Why** is it important?
- **How** you will identify ways to measure success.

Use verbs in your plan because no goal can be achieved without action.

What is an important goal for me?

What is my plan?

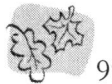

"If you struggle with getting enough Zzz's, try taking 5-HTP (5-Hydroxtryptophan), which may help boost serotonin levels to aid sleep."

~ Mehmet Oz, MD
(DoctorOz.com)

Fall

Day Forty-five

Terms in the Company of Pain
5-Hydroxytryptophan (5-HTP)

5-HTP is a form of the tryptophan, which is an essential amino acid that our body converts to the neurotransmitter serotonin. It may increase levels of serotonin that works to ease depression, modulate pain, and improve sleep patterns.

> *neurotransmitter = a relay chemical that carries, boosts and creates harmony between neurons (nerve cells) and other cells in the body.

Take this supplement only under the supervision of your doctor. Even though 5-HTP is sold over the counter, it can heighten effects or interfere with effects of other medications or disorders.

(You can read more on other supplements in the other books in this series.)

"By learning to collect our own data, acquiring effective communication skills, we can take a major role in the outcome of our physical and mental well-being."

Excerpt, *Integrative Therapies for Fibromyalgia, Chronic Fatigue Syndrome, and Myofascial Pain: The Mind-Body Connection"* by Celeste Cooper, RN and Jeff Miller, PhD Press

🙦 Fall 🙤
Day Forty-six

How to Avoid Being a Space Cadet
Learning to Communicate with Your Healthcare Provider

Over the past decade or so, patients have taken on a new role in their healthcare. We are now expected to be involved, whereas in the past, we experienced an authoritative type of communication from our physicians. Studies tell us that many physicians, unless they have taken a course on communication skills, still have difficulty with this important piece, and this piece is important to all of us because we know effective communication between physician and patient improves outcomes. Following are tips and expectations for improving our skills.

Seven tips for effective communication:

1. Have an agenda.
2. Assume a position of comfort.
3. Establish eye contact.
4. Listen without interrupting.
5. Show attention with nonverbal cues, such as nodding.
6. Confirm what you think you hear.
7. Allow expression of feelings.

A good patient communicator will:

- Have an agenda that meets the allotted time.
- Be prepared to report on success or failure of previous treatment.
- Understand that the doctor sees more than one patient and may need to reschedule to meet all of your needs.
- Ask questions that are specific to symptoms.
- Listen to the doctor's answer and take a quick note if possible.
- Ask for clarification of the treatment plan when needed.
- Understand the doctor should be respectful and willing to listen. (Everyone has a bad day, but if the behavior continues, it's time to move on.)
- Restate the results of the appointment so neither you nor the doctor miss anything important.

(See more on communication in the *Summer Devotions* of this series.

What things can I do to improve my communication with my healthcare provider?

_____

_____

_____

Notes

Defeat is a possibility of try, but to quit scars the soul.

~Celeste

~ Fall ~
Day Forty-seven

Is the Yin in Your Yang?
Evaluating Therapies and Treatments

The goal of all therapies and treatments should be to relieve pain and fatigue, and improve function.

How to evaluate therapeutic effects:

- Does the therapy improve function, and if so, by what percent?
- Does the therapy interfere with function, and if so, how, and by what percent?
- Do you engage in therapy as prescribed? If not, why not?
- Do you manage self-therapy, such as Yoga, T'ai Chi, Qi Gong, Pilates, meditation, stretching, or biofeedback?
- Do you share success and failure of alternative therapies with your physician?

Sometimes we forget to share with our doctor what we do at home to improve our function. Be sure to share these things with your doctor. A comprehensive approach is most successful.

How are my therapies working for me?

"Every now and again take a good look at something not made with hands —a mountain, a star, the turn of a stream. There will come to you wisdom and patience and solace and, above all, the assurance that you are not alone in the world."

~Sidney Lovett, 1890 – 1979,
renowned chaplain at Yale University

❧ Fall ❧

Day Forty-eight

Follow Your Passion

It is easy to become passionate about people we admire or things we love.

I love:

- Having a positive role model.
- Nature.
- The grandeur of a mountain.
- A good cup of herbal tea.
- A stream that speaks.
- Birds that sing.
- Sharing information with people.
- Having a network.
- A path less traveled.
- Advocating for others and myself.
- A friend who shows mutual respect.

Start an "I love" list on one of the empty spots in this book, see where it takes you, you will be pleased.

(See "Day Seventy-five," and find more exercises throughout the *Broken Body, Wounded Spirit…* series.)

I love …

*"An intimate relationship is one that
allows you to be yourself"*

– Deepak Chopra, MD,
mind-body medicine expert, and author,
The Book of Secrets, Reinventing the Body, and more...

Fall

Day Forty-nine

Intimacy and Loyalty
Finding Sustenance

It is important for those of us in chronic pain to have supportive relationships. Loyal family and friends are an important aspect of our personal growth and help us move away from the focus of pain.

A good supporter is a person we like, respect, and trust. We share common interests with a good friend, and we experience a positive connection if the relationship is healthy. A loyal companion is someone we can share anything with and feel safe. Our relationships should be comfortable and relaxed, making us feel at ease. It is important is to be free of judging or being judged, and while keeping in touch by phone or email is important, we can share face-to-face time too.

These things are what we look for in others and what others should look for in us. A sustained relationship or friendship is one of mutual respect.

What do I look for in a supportive relationship?

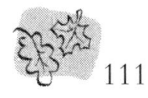

"Pay attention to your body. The point is everybody is different. You have to figure out what works for you."

~Andrew Weil, MD, integrative health expert and author of
True Food, Spontaneous Happiness, and more...

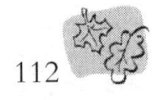

Fall
Day Fifty

Terms in the Company of Pain
Glucosamine and Chondroitin

Diseases that affect the joints can often be a source of chronic pain. Glucosamine and chondroitin, separately or combined, have similar actions for benefiting joint health.

Glucosamine is a supplement primarily for people with degenerative osteoarthritis. It is thought to decrease pain and improve mobility, and it may help repair damaged cartilage (the elastic tissue that lines joints, lubricates, and functions as a shock absorber.)

Chondroitin sulfate is a compound that is believed to block the enzymes that destroy cartilage tissue.

The body uses glucosamine to help make chondroitin. Therefore, whether taken together or alone, each can play a role in improving joint mobility and slowing cartilage loss.

*There are also some general interactions and precautions between glucosamine and other medications, so check with your doctor or pharmacist before taking it.

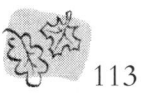

"History has demonstrated that the most notable winners usually encountered heartbreaking obstacles before they triumphed. They won because they refused to become discouraged by their defeats."

~B. C. Forbes

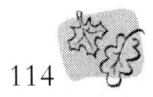

Fall
Day Fifty-one

Being a Mover and a Shaker
Hints for Safe Exercise

Getting up and moving is important to our health. It not only helps our body release feel good hormones called endorphins, it improves our immune system, our circulation, and our heart health. Moving is the only thing that keeps the lymph system functioning and prevents cellular waste from stagnation. Having a problem with your disposition? Get up and move, because it improves our mood. The type of movement or exercise should be one we enjoy, but there are certain rules that are of particular importance to those of us who live with chronic pain.

Tips for moving safely:

- Start slowly and carefully to build tolerance.
- Address aggravating factors before beginning.
- Warm up in a warm shower or do gentle stretches before starting.
- Vary your movements.
- Provide a cool down period by gently stretching your muscles after exercise.
- Wear non-restrictive clothing and footwear.

- Exercise at a time of day when you have the least amount of pain and stiffness.
- Avoid nighttime exercise.
- Provide yourself with adequate rest periods.
- Practice abdominal breathing and relaxation.
- Try low impact aerobic exercise, such as aquatic therapy or walking.
- Drink plenty of water after aggressive movement.
- Cool down with gentle stretching.
- Remember, more may not always be better; assess, and address.
- Wait at least one hour after eating before exercising.

(Read more on exercise and movement therapies in the other books in this series and specifics on aerobic exercise in *Summer Devotions.*)

What are things I can do to keep me safe when I exercise?

Notes

Learning is my arsenal against pain and spirit my greatest armor.

~Celeste

Fall

Day Fifty-two

Investigative Reporter

Making the Headlines for Our Own Symptoms

What is that nagging sensation that we can't put our finger on? Many describe this as our sixth sense; the instinct that tells us there is an intruder afoot. The intruder is pain and fatigue, and they sometimes change our ability to think straight. Here are some tips for investigation:

- Keep a calendar of symptoms and activities.
- Identify activity, medication, and food or sleep patterns that aggravate symptoms.
- Identify what helps most.
- Are there other conditions that make pain worse?
- What's your posture like?
- Do you critically assess your ability to get up and move?
- Does moving make symptoms better or worse?
- Do certain foods make symptoms worse?
- Are you listening to your body talk?

This feeling will nag us to keep going until we find an explanation.

How can I hone in on my investigative skills?

"I've learned....
That being kind is more important than being right. "

~Andy Rooney

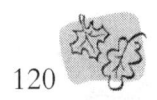

Fall

Day Fifty-three

If I Can't Be Kind, I Need to Zip It!

This is great advice given to me by Jeff, the other author of this book. It is a simple exercise to remember when brainfog from sleep deprivation, medications, or the nature of our illness steps in. These three little sentences can make a BIG change in our life. Share them; this little pyramid works for everybody.

Before acting on thoughts or feelings, do a quick assessment.

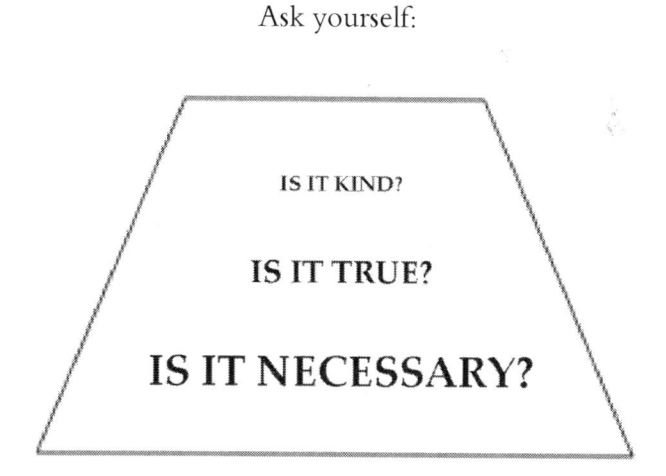

Ask yourself:

IS IT KIND?

IS IT TRUE?

IS IT NECESSARY?

I will copy this for my journal or have it framed to hang on the wall.

"*Happiness is a butterfly, which when pursued,
is always just beyond your grasp, but which,
if you sit down quietly, may alight upon you.*"

~Nathaniel Hawthorne, 1804 – 1864

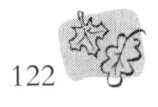

~ Fall ~

Day Fifty-four

Just for the Heck of It!

Spontaneity is not something we have to plan; it comes naturally.

When we do something for someone else, "just for the heck of it," without reason, not expecting anything in return, we are rewarded in immeasurable ways. It doesn't have to be something elaborate or costly.

Surprise somebody you care about and enjoy the outcome.

- Greet your significant other, barely clad.
- Tell a stranger they have a pretty smile when you notice it.
- Surprise your children or pets.
- Hug somebody.
- Don't forget to say thank you.
- Help a neighbor with a task that is particularly difficult for them, such as navigating a customer service recording.

What is something I can do spontaneously for someone else?

*Accepting can sometimes be the hardest thing we face,
but often, the first step to understanding.*

~Celeste

Fall

Day Fifty-five

Terms in the Company of Pain
Any Other Pain: The "A" in Pain

acupuncture = an ancient Chinese method for pain treatment using needles and specific mapped meridians.

agonist = helper, works with.

algia = painful condition

algology = the science and study of pain.

allodynia = known as *other pain*, meaning pain from stimuli that are not normally painful.

analgesia = the absence of pain response to a type of stimulation that normally would be painful.

antagonist = counteracts, works against

arth = prefix denoting joint involvement.

arthralgia = joint pain; pain where two bones meet.

Do I have other "A" words to add to this list?

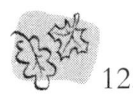

"I can be changed by what happens to me.
But I refuse to be reduced by it."

-Maya Angelou

Fall

Day Fifty-six

Beware of the Tangled Web

Chronic pain lures us to try just about anything to relieve our misery. Be careful not to be bitten by those who would take advantage of our circumstances for their own secondary gain.

Beware if:

- An ad suggests it is a "miracle cure."
- An ad suggests a treatment is backed by scientific evidence, but they do not provide references to the research.
- A preparation does not have a contact name listed on the label.
- It is a steroid or other hormonal preparation. Your doctor should check your own hormone levels to determine if you need this.
- The practitioner says he or she can cure an illness that no one else can.
- The practitioner avoids showing credentials.
- The practitioner demands you sign a financial contract for services instead of listening to your complaint.
- The practitioner intimidates you or puts you on the defensive.

How can I avoid the tangled web?

"Two roads diverged in a wood…
I took the one less traveled by,
and that has made all the difference."

~Robert Frost, American poet, 1874-1963

❧ Fall ❧
Day Fifty-seven

Goals for the Soul Day

Like achieving any goal, we need a plan. Following are a few tips for becoming more spiritual.

- See the good.
- Wag more; bark less.
- Practice prayer and meditation.
- Become more open to achieving spiritual awareness.
- Focus on the good of humankind.
- Seek spiritual fellowship.
- Embrace the healing qualities of spirituality.
- Find or write a spiritual affirmation for yourself, and commit it to memory by saying or reading it regularly.
- Know spirituality is an important element of wellness.
- Accept your higher good.

When we use these tips to change our focus, it improves our overall feeling of well-being, giving us balance.

(Learn about spiritual journaling in the *Spring Devotions*.)

My spiritual goals are...

Frowning wrinkles the spirit.

~Celeste

Fall

Day Fifty-eight

Dosing the Laughter Medicine

Laughter is truly an exercise. It flexes the diaphragm, chest, and abdominal muscles, and causes us to breathe deeply. It helps us relax, and it increases the production of endorphins that help to relieve pain.

- Let laughter be your weapon against pain.
- Share a good joke. (Write it down if you need to.)
- Be able to laugh at yourself, every day.
- Make laughter contagious.
- Laugh out loud for no reason.
- Feel your spirits lift and the tension resolve when you laugh.

> "You don't stop laughing because you grow old; you grow old because you stop laughing."
>
> ~unknown

(Because laughter is so important to our mental, emotional, spiritual, and physical health, some aspect is included in all the books in this series.)

I will laugh today.

The experience of pain creates a sense of duty to help others sharing my cobblestone path. I may not be physically sure footed, but I am certain of vision.

~Celeste

Fall
Day Fifty-nine

Chaos and Clutter
The Disaster Plan

Physical and mental clutter breed chaos, making it very important to keep our environment organized. When we are organized, we have fewer choices, which help with mental clarity and it promotes less anxiety. Following are some tips for getting and staying organized:

- Know your in-box.
- Practice the "in-out rule." When something new comes in something old goes out.
- Put things back from whence they came.
- Keep frequently used items close by.
- Label things.
- Keep things simple.
- When in need, ask for help.

Clutter can also be a safety hazard, particularly for those of us who are more like a bull in a china cabinet. By keeping things picked up and organized, we are less likely to take a nosedive into the proverbial brick wall.

How and why should I get organized?

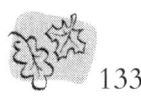

"Pain is the duality of pleasure."

~Jack Kornfield , PhD, author and teacher,
*A Path with Heart, the Wise Heart:
A Guide to the Universal Teachings of Buddhist Psychology*, and more...

Fall

Day Sixty

Terms in the Company of Pain
Serotonin

Serotonin, also called hydroxytriptamine, is one of two key chemicals in pain messaging, the other, ironically, is substance P. Serotonin plays an important role in neurotransmission.

> Neurotransmission is the squawk box, the Walkie Talkie(TM) that keeps communication going between the brain and the body.

This important amino acid, serotonin, is stored in the brain but it is also present in the blood, central nervous system and other tissues. Produced enzymatically from tryptophan, it is also important for stimulating smooth muscle found in our organs.

Serotonin is known as one of the "feel good" chemicals, and low levels of serotonin have been attributed to poor mood, the expression of pain, and repressed sleep.

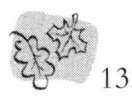

"The mighty oak was once
a little nut that stood its ground."

~Unknown

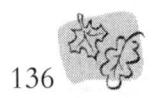

❧ Fall ❧

Day Sixty-one

Omega–3

Derived from fish oil, Omega 3 (EPA and DHA) is thought to reduce pain, stabilize mood, and possibly reduce cholesterol. According to cardiologist and Assistant Professor of Medicine at Columbia University, Dr Ozden Dogan, "Omega-3 has anti-inflammatory effects that keep our blood vessels healthy. It increases nitric oxide, an excellent chemical that makes our vessels bigger so more blood can be sent to our heart. It prevents irregular heartbeat, and it is an anticoagulant that can prevent blockages in the blood vessels that can lead to heart attack or stroke." (Sharecare.com)

It is evident that, because of its anti-inflammatory qualities, Omega 3 also has an effect on conditions that cause chronic pain.

Talk with your doctor about the benefits of Omega-3 for you.

Always purchase supplements from a reputable dealer to avoid harmful contaminants.

*May your kindness supply an abundant harvest.
May you find your reflection in every soul you meet.
May the grace you share create tenderness in you.*

~Celeste

❧ Fall ❧
Day Sixty-two

Does Your Belly Button Sag?
(Metaphorically speaking)

The umbilical cord signifies the core of life. Metaphorically, it is our life source for soulfulness and self-reflection. It is by grace that we are given an abundance of opportunities.

What one word best describes your belly button?

- adventurous
- creative
- dependable
- dutiful
- flexible
- honest
- intelligent
- kind
- patient
- responsible
- sincere
- soulful
- trustworthy
- unselfish
- valuable
- wise

Don't stop now. Drag out your journal or write here, right now, in this book. Make a list of your own words that signifies what you feel is at your core. Think pleasant thoughts as you write down your words. If you are drawn off course, that's okay, just bring yourself back to your list. You will be glad you did this exercise.

What words can I use as suspenders for my belly button?

_____
_____
_____
_____
_____
_____
_____
_____
_____

Smile!

Notes

Away from the speech of illness, my vocabulary consists of life affirming words—courage, determination, wisdom, faith, harmony and hope.

~Celeste

Fall

Day Sixty-three

Aggravation Gives Me Attitude

It's easy to become annoyed when our body doesn't respond the way we would like it to respond. However, there are aggravating factors that, when controlled, give us feelings of accomplishment, and improves our mood making us feel better about our circumstances.

Here are a few suggestions for improving your attitude:

- Identify known stressors, particularly on a stress-ridden day.
- Respond with a resounding no to negative thoughts.
- Employ your stop word or phrase. Mine is "Let go."
- Change your friends if necessary.
- Be positive with your body; give it the tender loving care it needs.
- Manage co-existing conditions.
- Nurture mutually rewarding relationships.
- Practice affirmations on a regular basis. (See "Day Seven.")
- Somebody else's stuff is their stuff; you are only responsible for your stuff.
- Take out your mental trash. (See *Summer Devotions.*)
- Monitor your internal dialogue. (See *Summer Devotions.*)

How can I change my "tude?"

"If you know how to worry, you already know how to meditate. Worry is negatively focused meditation."

—Rick Warren, Evangelical Christian minister and author of *The Purpose Driven Life, What on Earth Am I Here For?* and more...

❧ *Fall* ❦

Day Sixty-four

Lay Your Worries Aside, Worrywart!

Worry doesn't solve problems. Instead, it creates a circle of negative feedback to the brain, which creates unnecessary stress. A train wreck will happen if we don't slow down at the crossings, and stop at the flashing light.

Remember:

- Worry will derail healthy coping strategies.
- Drama is only good in the movies.
- We have no control over other people's stuff.
- We can create positive energy by changing focus.
- We can only control how WE deal with things.
- Train wrecks happen.
- Worrying over something that hasn't happened says we can predict the future—not rational.

It's human to worry, but being human gives us free will. When we let worry dominate, we easily succumb to the destructive energy of anxiety, apprehension, and depression. We do better when we let go of worry as our "go to" coping strategy.

What stop word can I use when I am a worrywart?

"The ultimate measure of a man is not where he stands in moments of comfort, but where he stands at times of challenge and controversy."

~Martin Luther King Jr.

~ Fall ~

Day Sixty-five

Having Pain Isn't Simple

In our society, we are often measured by what we do for a living; when that is threatened, it affects both our personal financial circumstances and our emotional health. However, when the condition that causes our pain or chronic pain itself limits our ability to remain in the work force, we can feel like we are out on a limb, isolated and fearful of what comes next.

The Social Security process for obtaining disability is daunting. Using an attorney who specializes in these claims vastly increases the odds you will succeed on appeal, and generally, they are held to a certain fee schedule. Since success for winning your appeal depends upon the attorney's ability to understand how pain affects your life, it is important to keep the documentation tools offered throughout this book series handy.

Don't let anyone tell you that you don't have the right to your benefits, because if they were in your situation, they would do the same, even if they think otherwise.

You have rights; remember that.

I may wear out, but I won't break down.

~Celeste

❧ Fall ☙

Day Sixty-six

Is It Time for a Check-up?
(circle those that apply)

My pain is:
Absent – tolerable – moderate – severe

My activity level is:
good – moderate – poor – very poor

My energy is:
good – moderate – poor – very poor

My sleep quality is:
good – moderate – poor – very poor

My sleep amount is:
2-4 hours   4-6 hours   6-8 hours   9 or more

I feel rested:
always – occasionally – never

My concentration/memory is:
good – moderate – poor – very poor

"Enlightenment is not knowledge that is learned but a state one must enter and become."

~Deepak Chopra, MD,
mind-body expert and author of
Brotherhood, Stress Free with Deepak Chopra, and more...

Fall

Day Sixty-seven

Enlightenment

Enlightenment is about becoming fully awake. It is a spiritual quest for learning to silence the mind and open the heart.

Obstacles to enlightenment include:

- Holding on to one's ego.
- Clinging to the idea that money brings happiness.
- Not being able to exercise patience. (See "Day Ninety" and *Summer Devotions*.)
- Walling yourself off to self-realization and mindfulness. (See "Day Ten" and *Spring Devotions*.)
- Harboring anger and fear.
- Unwillingness to put forth the effort.
- Expecting an explanation, or not having faith.
- Failing to see opportunity in adversity.
- Ignoring the concept that all living things have purpose.
- Standing in judgment.
- Not being able to forgive yourself.

We have a better chance of enlightened, when we address these obstacles.

How can I live an enlightenment, aware, and mindful life?

FALL DEVOTIONS, authors Cooper & Miller

*I observe the beauty of life and
the teachings of the passage.*

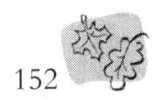

~Celeste

🍂 Fall 🍂
Day Sixty-eight

Terms in the Company of Pain
Kinesiology

Kinesiology is a diagnostic system based on the premise that individual muscle functions provide information about a patient's overall health. Practitioners test the strength and mobility of certain muscles, analyze a patient's posture and gait, and inquire about lifestyle factors that may be contributing to an illness. A skilled practitioner also knows to look for any underlying symptoms that have not become a serious problem so they can address them beforehand.

Most people experiencing chronic pain have a myofascial component. (See *Spring* and *Summer Devotions*.) The muscles, bones, and attachments of our joints are responsible for our ability to move about. Understanding how everything works together is important for easing pain and dysfunction.

Nutrition, muscle and joint manipulation, diet and exercise are included as part of a treatment plan. Licensed professionals, including, chiropractors, physical therapists, dentists, medical doctors (MDs) and doctors of osteopathy (DOs) all practice kinesiology.

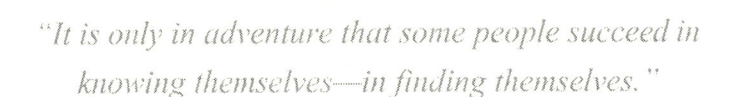

"It is only in adventure that some people succeed in knowing themselves—in finding themselves."

~André Gide, 1869 – 1951.
French author and winner of the Nobel Prize in literature.

Fall

Day Sixty-nine

All Hail to the Dropped Ball

We develop ways to cope as an act of self-preservation, but sometimes we aren't aware that our behavior is blocking our growth, we may think quite the opposite. Everybody drops the ball, so this is an opportunity to hit a home run when others may be stuck on first base.

- How do you think others describe you?
- Do you expect others to play by your rules?
- Do you tend to slough off, when you can do more?
- Do you let anxiety or depression set your pace?
- Do you make excuses when in conflict, avoidance, or feeling isolated?
- Do you use the silent treatment when you should talk things out?
- Are you overly critical of others or yourself?
- Do you accept that pain is part of your person, but it does not define your character?
- Do you have negative internal dialogue?
- Do you accept there is learning in mistakes?
- Do you accept that nobody is perfect?
- Do you accept that everybody drops the ball sometimes?

What blocks can I admit to myself today?

Verbs once foremost in my vocabulary, push, strive, excel, have been replaced with baby steps, one day at a time, your best is good enough.

~Celeste

Fall

Day Seventy

Has My Piggy Bank Been Robbed?

Every day, we should spend down to our last penny (available energy tokens) but not one cent more. One extra penny expended today will cost the chronic pain patient a dollar tomorrow! We need to make daily deposits in our well-being bank. This requires unwavering assessment of our abilities. We need to keep this limit sacrosanct.

While assessing our abilities and avoiding self-deception, we need to do a balancing act with our unconscious process of assessing our abilities and avoiding self-trickery. This course of action is a characteristic we all experience. It is our allowance and consent to loaf, stall, or non-perform. This tendency to give up prematurely, surrender to dread, or fall short of our goals is universal. That's right, universal; it doesn't only apply to people in pain.

By not overextending or underperforming, we decrease the risk of unbalance. Stay focused. Something can always be done to help us avoid robbing our energy reserves blind.

Is my piggy bank busting at the seams or am I in debt?

"Courage is resistance to fear, mastery of fear—not
absence of fear. Except a creature be part coward,
it is not a compliment to say he is brave;
it is merely a loose misapplication of the word."

~Mark Twain, Samuel Clemens
(Pudd'nhead Wilson's Calendar)

❧ Fall ❧
Day Seventy-one

Pain vs. Suffering

While eliminating pain may not be possible, reducing suffering is. The goal of talking with a good therapist when we have chronic pain is to improve the quality of our life by identifying and changing the elements that keep us stuck. A psychotherapist might be a psychologist, counselor, or social worker.

Keys to finding the right counselor include:

- Someone in your healthcare or insurance network.
- Someone easily accessible to your geographical area.
- Someone who is licensed by your state.
- Someone that was referred to you.
- A personal level of comfort.
- Appropriate expectations.
- A sense of mutual trust.
- Specific and personal goals.
- Someone who uses various therapeutic approaches.
- Someone experienced in treating people with chronic pain.

Could talk therapy be right for me?

*Acceptance can be the hardest thing we face,
but without it, we can't change our perception.*

~Celeste

Fall

Day Seventy-two

Is My Cranium Stuck in Overdrive?
Biofeedback

Biofeedback is a tool that tells us how our body reacts in times of perceived stress. It helps us identify specific personal relaxation techniques to calm down our body's reaction to pain. This reaction is an adaptive fight or flight response that raises our blood pressure and heart rate and puts undue and unnecessary tension on our body.

Restricted breathing due to pain, injury, tender points, or trigger points can result in a decreased ability to provide oxygen to our cells. Oxygen is necessary for cellular health and for healing, and biofeedback can be a helpful accessory to improving how we breathe. You can read more about the healing power of breathing in *Fall Devotions*.

Biofeedback is non-invasive that uses technology to monitor our physical responses, such as heart rate, skin conductivity of electricity, muscle tension, respiration, or brain waves, so we can voluntarily change our physical state toward a more balanced being.

Is biofeedback something I might like to try?

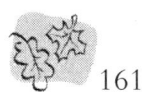

"Until you stop breathing,
there's more right with you than wrong with you."

~Jon Kabat-Zinn, author of
Letting Everything Become Your Teacher,
Full Catastrophe Living, and more...

Fall

Day Seventy-three

To Inspire or to Expire

We all know we have to breathe to escape permanent expiration, but we must know how to get the biggest bang for our buck. Not only is diaphragmatic breathing a good relaxation tool, it also improves oxygen intake, which is the fuel source for all our body's cells. It's easy and it's free!

When our diaphragm is not relaxing, it can impede the capacity for oxygen rich air. So how do we relax our diaphragm? We "belly breathe." It is best to start your practice with loose clothing and an empty stomach. We all know how hard it can be to breathe with a belt too tight or when we overeat.

Lay on the bed/ floor on your back; now, put one piece of paper on your belly and one on your chest. When you inhale, the paper on your belly should rise further than the one on your chest. Exhaling is natural and takes no effort; however, for newbies, try tightening your tummy muscles as you exhale. Practice makes perfect

Do I feel calmer now?

*I have favorite words, because I love the impact
they have on my attitude as I write them down.*

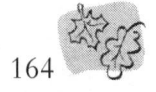

~Celeste

❧ Fall ❧

Day Seventy-four

Verbosity: Action Words to Play With and Live By

Action words to play with and live by:

- accepting
- achieving
- affirming
- creating
- exploring
- challenging
- giving
- thanking
- helping
- journaling
- learning
- laughing
- practicing
- praising
- nurturing
- willing

If you listen to the Dr. Phil show, you have heard him say at least a hundred times, "Put verbs in your sentences." He says this for a very important reason. Verbs are what make us spring into action.

All aspects of a plan whatever it may be, including the "Crisis Plan" discussed earlier has "verbosity." Every goal, our plans to achieve it, the steps we take to implement it, and even our evaluation and reassessment always includes verbs. So sit down now, you probably already are, and list some verbs that you can make important to your life.

I will identify and put two of my new ideas into a sentence and tape them to my mirror.

Notes

*I wrote this poem from a random list of things I like.
Focusing on positives is important to me and so is poetry.
It blended so easily, I almost feel guilty.*

~Celeste

Fall

Seventy-five

The Promise of Like *by Celeste Cooper*

I like camping, picnics, mountains with streams,
Invading my space and into my dreams,
Loony family, self, friends, and birds,
Even failing to speak with words.

Fortune to learn, watching children at play,
Scenery, lakes that reflect on the day,
Cakes, spirituality, flowers, a good book,
And cactus that wink with a special look.

Mixed sun, the fall's rain, a cloud that churns
Laughter, antiques, Hummels, and urns,
Gentle music, dogs, sea horses, and cats,
Wildlife inspires me even the bats.

I like promise and hope, flowers I like
I like beginnings and endings, I just like

What are some of my favorite words?

I will write my own "I like" poem.

*Movement of a single rock can change the
course of a river forever.*

~Celeste

Fall

Day Seventy-six

Terms in the Company of Pain
Homeostasis

Homeostasis is a tendency of our body to maintain stability by constantly adjusting to conditions that threaten the balance that is mandatory for survival. This tendency is seen throughout all things. For instance, if a rockslide covers a river, the river will adjust and change its course, but it will keep flowing.

We learned earlier that the chronic pain state puts an extraordinary amount of pressure on this system but homeostasis still manages to keep things flowing despite challenges. It is important to remember that our body, like that river, is always set in survival mode no matter what comes its way. Knowing that our body is always under the pressure to maintain balance should raise our awareness and appreciation for all it does to keep things in order. Changing course for survival is a good thing and if we change one thought word in response to pain, it is a gift of appreciation we can give our body.

What one rock in my thinking can I change?

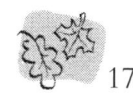

The impotence of pain to create a positive force is counterbalanced by strength of mind and a sense of duty and vision.

~Celeste

❦ Fall ❧

Day Seventy-seven

Terms in the Company of Pain

The 'I's in Pain:

Because pain is personal, it is important to convey to our care providers exactly how our pain feels to us. We can do this by using words that paint a clear picture. Following are a few "I" words we might use to describe our pain.

- immobilizing
- impairing
- incapacitating
- incinerating
- incessant
- in knots
- intense
- intermittent
- internal
- intolerable
- incapacitating
- irritating

Words I use to describe my symptoms are:

"Begin to know yourself as something far greater than the ever changing, ever dying aspects that have dominated your picture of who you are."

~ Wayne W. Dyer, PhD, author of
I am Wishes Fulfilled Meditation,
The Power of Intention, and more...

❧ Fall ☙

Day Seventy-eight

All aboard the Soul Train
Exploring Creative Visualization

The practice of creative visualization can help us cope with physical, emotional, or spiritual pain. The goal is to refocus attention on other stimuli that helps us begin the process of correction.

Creative visualization is similar to guided imagery and can be done on your own or with the guidance of a CD or trained therapist.

Here are some tips:

- Identify your creative self, talents, personal skills, and gifts and use them during your practice.
- Note the feel, look, and texture of your body parts that are in pain.
- Examine your pain without judging it.
- Have a dialogue with a painful body part and imagine the pain in colors.
- Now, visualize the transformation of pain to a soft colorful pastel that will eventually be erased and released by your own creative energy.

Remember, without intention, our mind will start to wander off course. This is a normal reaction. We are not to judge; we are to recognize it as a neutral party. When we are able to do this, we can give our body the tenderness it deserves; after all, it didn't ask for pain anymore than we did.

I will practice this often and visualize my body healing.

Notes

"I've learned.... that having a child fall asleep in your arms is one of the most peaceful feelings in the world."

~Andy Rooney

❧ Fall ❧

Day Seventy-nine

Through a Child's Eyes...

Looking through the eyes of a child is an experience of wonder, questioning, acceptance, and imagination. Do you remember how you saw the world as a child?

How do you remember yourself? What did you enjoy doing when you were growing up? Do you remember anyone in particular that made you feel important? Were there any particularly painful moments to acknowledge and let go? (If you answered yes to that last question, and if the painful experience was significant enough to keep you from moving forward with this exercise, please see a qualified therapist to help you work through it.)

Seeing ourselves through a child's eyes in a positive way can help us reclaim that part of who we are as individuals.

I will write a short story about a positive experience from my childhood.

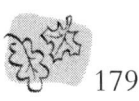

*To be unlimited in thinking is to see the world at
my front door, ready to explore.*

~Celeste

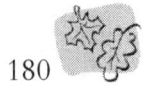

🍂 Fall 🍂
Day Eighty

Integration in Combination

Sometimes we feel our healthcare provider is at a loss because chronic pain is complex. Therefore, we often consider integrative or complementary therapies. Some well-researched integrative healing practices may help. Following are some suggestions.

- Take a class or pick up a DVD on Qigong or T'ai Chi.
- Explore the MANY relaxation techniques available, such as creative visualization on *Day Seventy-eight* or mindfulness exercises in *Spring* and *Summer Devotions*.
- Practice movement therapies on a regular basis. (Moving is the only thing that keeps the lymph system working.)
- Get out in fresh air and natural light for 20 minutes a day.

Many integrative practices can be self-taught. Check out your local library; explore the teachings of wise people.

> *"A very great vision is needed and the man who has it must follow it as the eagle seeks the deepest blue of the sky."*
>
> ~Crazy Horse, Sioux Chief

How can I integrate some practices into my plan for balance?

"Internally generated states project as external reality."

– Deepak Chopra, MD,
mind-body medicine expert, and author of
Super Brain, The Seven Spiritual Laws of Success, and more...

~ Fall ~

Day Eighty-one

Lining up Bats in Your Belfry

Many people in chronic pain complain of brainfog making it more difficult to get organized, but this is when we need to do it the most. Following are a few hints to help us get organized:

- Don't hoard.
- Arrange tasks in small increments.
- Keep your "things" in one place.
- Have one calendar to live by. Put it in a central location so household members can refer to it too.
- Have your own special area.
- Keep frequently used items handy. You will be more inclined to use that topical ointment, theracane, neck pillow, massager, word games, puzzles, etc.
- Clear out mind clutter, and write things down.
- Exercise your brainpower, set priorities.
- Keep things simple.
- Ask for help.

When our physical environment is disorganized, it can contribute to mental clutter and make coping more difficult.

What can I organize today?

"*Things that were hard to bear are sweet to remember.*"

~Lucius Annacus Seneca, 4 BC – 65 AD,
Philosopher and Statesman

❧ Fall ❧
Day Eighty-two

Flapping the Wings of Our Brain Cells
Improving Our Senior Moments

Tips for exercising your brain to keep it healthy:

- Exercise regularly.
- Be social.
- Play word games.
- Play number games.
- Memorize words to an old song.
- Memorize one of the poems in this book.
- Scan your doctor's office lobby, then write down everything you remember seeing while you're waiting in the exam room.
- Listen to an audio book while doing another task.
- Eat healthy and avoid complex carbohydrates. (See *Spring* and *Winter Devotions* for tips on food choices and their effect on health, and how to track food related symptoms.)
- Brush your teeth in the dark.

Practices for mental clarity will help bring balance to the body.

What can I do today to avoid losing brain cells?

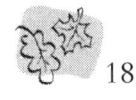

Physical pain has no boundaries, so I choose to view it through my binoculars. It is there, I can see it, but if I keep it in the distance, it is only visible if I magnify it.

~Celeste

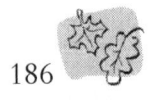

❧ Fall ❧

Day Eighty-three

Concerns to Consider

When dealing with pain, we may have concerns. Following are questions to consider.

- Are we afraid of what we might discover?
- Are we able to afford medications?
- Are past-experiences limiting our trust?
- Will treating symptoms get to the root cause?
- How do we recognize, treat, and control underlying conditions?
- Are we identifying aggravating factors correctly?
- Are we able to maintain good posture?
- Could ill-fitting garments be aggravators?
- Do we have a metabolic disorder that might interfere with our progress?
- Do we know our food triggers?
- Is sleep quality intruding on pain?
- Is poor sleep hygiene a factor?
- Do we dwell on thoughts over which we have no control?

Once we identify our concerns, we can set reasonable goals.

How do any of these concerns apply to me?

"Pain pays the income of each precious thing."

~William Shakespeare

❧ Fall ❦

Day Eighty-four

Does "My Device" Mean My Body?

It is important to stretch to maintain normal muscle length and function. It is something athletes do to warm up their muscles before a hike or a run. Physical therapists exercise the bedridden passively to deter muscle wasting.

We need to stretch and exercise, but we sometimes avoid them, because they cause pain. The less we do, the more pain we will be in, so move we must. Following are some cautions for stretching that when heeded will reduce the risk of causing more pain.

- Always start low and go slow, building tolerance gradually.
- Don't attempt to stretch immediately after coming in from the cold.
- Don't stretch after using therapeutic ice packs.
- Don't stretch to a point of maximum tension (ease off to about 70-80% effort).

The benefits of stretching are well known, so think about how you might incorporate stretching into routine tasks.

How can I incorporate a stretch throughout my day?

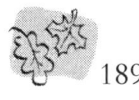

*Where we stand in times of adversity,
determines who we become.*

~Celeste

Fall

Day Eighty-five

Terms in the Company of Pain
The 'N's in Pain

neuralgia = pain in a nerve or along the course of a nerve track.

neuritis = inflammation of peripheral nerves including nerves associated with muscles, skin, organs, and all other parts of the body which link to the brain via the spinal cord nerve roots.

neuropathic pain = pain caused by a functional or pathological change in the peripheral nervous system.

neuropathy = disturbance of function or pathologic (not normal) change in a nerve.

nociceptor = a receptor preferentially sensitive to a noxious or prolonged noxious stimulus.

"*Give to every other human being
every right that you claim for yourself.*"

~Robert G. Ingersoll, 1833-1899

Fall
Day Eighty-six

Mindful Exercise

Mindful exercise is physical exercise plus a type of meditation that tells us to exclude trying to solve the problems. Instead, we should allow our thoughts to—just be. When we do this, our body will let go, and the exercise will be spiritual and soothing.

Moving meditation should be kept simple. We should focus on our breathing or a specific movement. We should watch our body as it moves and marvel in its functionality.

There are many forms of movement meditation, including T'ai Chi, Hatha Yoga, and more, but you don't have use a formal type if it's not something that sounds interesting for you. As long as you have a body and a mind, you can do your own mindfully executed exercise. If physical disabilities don't allow you to walk or move in other ways, you can do it from a seated position or from a rocking chair. It only requires moving and meditating, awareness without judgment...Imagine that!

Today I will journal my experience with this meditative practice.

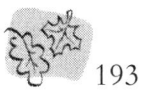

"To read without reflecting is like eating without digesting."

-Edmund Burke, 1729 – 1797,
Irish political philosopher, author, and orator

Fall

Day Eighty-seven

Curiosity Killed the Cat

It's human nature to be curious. We have all experienced the always present and universal conduct to slow down when there is an accident on the road. We do it because we are curious. While our motivations may differ, we don't always know exactly why we do it, we just do it. Even if we aren't the gawker, this time, someone invariably ties up traffic for the sake of having their curiosity satisfied. Ok, so we know we have this innate sense. The question is, "How can we learn from such instinctive behavior?"

Curiosity, wanting answers, is how we learn, but we won't learn a thing if we don't pause for the lesson. Understanding the motivation for curiosity helps define how sharing an experience might be useful. Don't we share accident stories because we hope to raise awareness of what can happen? We should make it a practice to be aware of our curious nature, to step in tune with our instincts. We might find we learn something new about someone or something when we take time to reflect. We might find new opportunities that could have a profound impact on our lives.

What new thing did I learn today?

Notes

Notes

"Friends are those rare people who ask how we are
and then wait to hear the answer."

~Ed Cunningham

Fall

Day Eighty-eight

Time for a Relationship Reminder

"Treasure your relationships, not your possessions"

~Anthony J. D'Angel,
Creator of *The Inspiration Book Series*

Close relationships are sometimes at risk when we are in pain. We run short on energy and can't always be there for others as much as we would like. Still, lasting relationships take commitment regardless of circumstances. To receive tolerance we should be willing to give it. We should be willing to nurture meaningful bonds, and every relationship deserves to be treated with the delicacy we would use to care for a newborn child or animal. Valued relationships become our treasures.

For relationships to survive we need to actively listen, we should "wait to hear the answer." Only heartfelt empathy will give us what we need in return. When we learn tolerance, we harvest the bounty of friendship, forgiveness, and grace.

What relationships do I wish to promote?

FALL DEVOTIONS, authors Cooper & Miller

*"There are only two ways to live your life.
One is as though nothing is a miracle.
The other is as if everything is."*

~Albert Einstein

❧ Fall ❧
Day Eighty-nine

Ayurvedic Medicine

Ayurvedic medicine is an ancient traditional medicine that considers the interaction between body, mind, and spirit. This medical philosophy employs the use of herbs, food, exercise, breathing, meditation, yoga, massage, and lifestyle change to restore balance.

In what ways can I balance my body, mind, and spirit?

"Have patience with all things, but chiefly have patience with yourself. Do not lose courage in considering your own imperfections, but instantly set about remedying them —every day begin the task anew."

~Saint Francis de Sales, 1567 – 1622

Fall

Day Ninety

Patience

We all have heard that patience is a virtue—virtue being wise, having merit and worth.

> *"When you get into a tight place and it seems you can't go on, hold on, for that's just the place and the time that the tide will turn."*
> ~Harriet Beecher Stowe

- Patience cannot be taught.
- Patience must be practiced.
- Patience fosters positive thought.
- Patience gives us staying power.
- Patience is a gift we give ourselves.
- Patience gives us fortitude.
- Patience is tolerance with one's self.
- Patience is waiting for the right time.
- Patience knows your triggers.
- Patience is the antidote for chaos.
- Patience is being present.
- Patience is letting go.
- Patience is waiting for the tide to turn.

Patience for me is ...

*"The butterfly counts not months
but moments, and has time enough."*

~Rabindranath Tagore, 1861-1941

❧ Fall ❧

Day Ninety-one

Affection

What better way to end this fall journey than to reflect of the words of one of the most sage people in American history, Samuel Clemmons, pen name Mark Twain.

> "Praise is well, compliment is well, but affection—that is the last and final and most precious reward that any man can win, whether by character or achievement."
>
> ~Mark Twain,
> Affection speech, 1907

I am the butterfly—I have time enough

Today I shall cherish someone I consider wise.

How can I use their insight as I transition my thoughts and actions from these fall gatherings into winter sustenance?

EPILOGUE

I have been to the end of the earth.

I have been to the end of the waters.

I have been to the end of the sky.

I have been to the end of the mountains.

I have found none that are not my friends.

-Navajo proverb

INDEX

Inside the Cover .... ii – iv

Acknowledgements vii

And We're Off ix

Introduction 1

Day One, The Native American Medicine Wheel 3

Day Two, Awaken senses 5

Day Three, Preparedness 7–8

Notes 9

Day Four, Exploring the Complements (CAM) 10

Day Five, Pondering My Uniqueness 12

Day Six, Willpower and Resolve 14

Day Seven, The Tree of Life—Affirmations 16

Day Eight, Learning from Our Experiences 18

Day Nine, Love in Poetry 20

Day Ten, Being Mindful of Our Thoughts and Body 22

Day Eleven, Chiropractic Medicine 24

Day Twelve, Speech is Not All Verbal. 26

Day Thirteen, Healthy Action Strategies 28

Notes 30–31

Day Fourteen, Being flexible 32

Day Fifteen, Revelations: The Big Reveal 34
Day Sixteen, Anxiety... 36
Day Seventeen, Managing Your Opportunities............... 38
Day Eighteen, Time for the "Periodic Review 40
Day Nineteen, Defining Triggers, Conquering Control... 42
Day Twenty, Challenging Your Brain Power 44
Day Twenty-one, Take a Stand............................... 46-48
Notes 49
Day Twenty-two, Tasks in Small Increments. 50
Day Twenty-three, Putting Stuff out to Pasture............. 52
Day Twenty-four, The 'P's in Pain 54
Day Twenty-five, Coming Front and Center 56
Day Twenty-six, Work that body, Trim Those Sails. 58
Day Twenty-seven, My Bridge 60
Day Twenty-eight, When in Crisis 62-64
Notes 65
Day Twenty-nine, The Activist...................................... 66
Day Thirty, Relationship Roulette................................. 68
Day Thirty-one, Spirituality.. 70
Day Thirty-two, Notions and Potions........................... 72

Day Thirty-three, Empowerment 74
Day Thirty-four, Kindness 76
Day Thirty-five, Journaling for Gold 78
Day Thirty-six, Chronic Pain 80-82
Notes 83
Day Thirty-seven, Karma 84
Day Thirty-eight, Challenge Yourself! 86
Day Thirty-nine, Clearing the Fog 88
Day Forty, We are a Package, the Whole Package. 90
Day Forty-one, Allopathic Medicine 92
Day Forty-two, Word Energy–Event Journaling 94
Day Forty-three, Neuralgia 96
Day Forty-four, Setting Goals 98
Day Forty-five, 5-Hydroxytryptophan (5-HTP) 100
Day Forty-six, A Good Patient Communicator 102-104
Notes 105
Day Forty-seven, Evaluating Therapies and Treatments . 106
Day Forty-eigh, Follow Your Passion. 108
Day Forty-nine, Supportive Relationships 110
Day Fifty, Glucosamine and Chondroitin 112

Day Fifty-one, Hints for Safe Exercise 114-116

Notes 117

Day Fifty-two, My Own Symptoms 118

Day Fifty-three, If I Can't Be Kind, I Need to Zip It! 120

Day Fifty-four, Spontaneity. 122

Day Fifty-five, Any Other Pain 124

Day Fifty-six, Beware of the Tangled Web. 126

Day Fifty-seven, Goals for the Soul Day 128

Day Fifty-eight, Dosing the Laughter Medicine 130

Day Fifty-nine, Chaos and clutter. 132

Day Sixty, Serotonin 134

Day Sixty-one, Omega-3 136

Day Sixty-two, Does Your Belly Button Sag? 138-140

Notes 141

Day Sixty-three, Aggravation Gives Me Attitude. 142

Day Sixty-four, Worry is Self-involved Negativity. 144

Day Sixty-five, Having Pain Isn't Simple. 146

Day Sixty-six, Is It Time for a Check-up? 148

Day Sixty-seven, Enlightenment 150

Day Sixty-eight, Kinesiology 152

Day Sixty-nine, All Hail to the Dropped Ball.................154

Day Seventy, Has My Piggy Bank Been robbed?...........156

Day Seventy-one, Pain vs. Suffering..........................158

Day Seventy-two, Biofeedback....................................160

Day Seventy-three, To Inspire or to Expire.................162

Day Seventy-four, Action words:.........................164-166

Notes...167

Day Seventy-five, The Promise of Like.......................168

Day Seventy-six, Homeostasis....................................170

Day Seventy-seven, Words to Describe the 'I's in PaIn:..172

Day Seventy-eight, Creative Visualization............174-176

Notes...177

Day Seventy-nine, Through a Child's Eyes..................178

Day Eighty, Integration in Combination.....................180

Day Eighty-one, Lining up Bats in Your Belfry............182

Day Eighty-two, Improving on Your Senior Moments..184

Day Eighty-three, Concerns to Consider......................186

Day Eighty-four, The Benefits of Stretching..................188

Day Eighty-five, The 'N's in Pain...............................190

Day Eighty-six, Mindful Exercise................................192

Day Eighty-seven, Curiosity. 194

Notes. 196-197

Day Eighty-eight, Time for a Relationship Reminder....198

Day Eighty-nine, Ayurvedic Medicine 200

Day Ninety, Patience 202

Day Ninety-one, Affection 204

EPILOGUE..206

ABOUT THE AUTHOR, Celeste Cooper, RN, BSN .214

ABOUT THE AUTHOR, Jeff Miller, PhD 216

Other books written by Cooper and Miller   218-221

ABOUT THE AUTHOR, Celeste Cooper, RN, BSN

Celeste Cooper is a retired advanced trained registered nurse who has transformed the way she copes with her own chronic pain. In her previous life, which she now thinks of as "before transformation," she was an educator, paralegal advisor, and caregiver. She received daily rewards from patients and students, and she appreciated the opportunity to be paid for something she loved to do. That all changed when overwhelming pain and chronic illness entered her life. She learned to navigate the road so many share with her, and she believes surviving the roadblocks, stumbles and all, have made her a better person. She feels fortunate to be able to use her time and talents with a purpose she believes is her legacy.

She is an advocate, and she is an expert on fibromyalgia at http://ShareCare.com an online health forum. She participates in the Pain Action Alliance to Implement a National Strategy, http://PAINSproject.org, which is an initiative of the Center for Practical Bioethics created to assist in the implementation of the Institute of Medicine report "Relieving Pain in America: A Blueprint for Transforming Prevention, Care, Education, and Research."

She is lead author of the 434-page book *Integrative Therapies for Fibromyalgia, Chronic Fatigue Syndrome, and Myofascial Pain: The Mind-Body Connection*, and *Broken Body, Wounded Spirit: Balancing the SeeSaw of Chronic Pain* four-book series. (See Other Books).

Celeste is committed to helping others turn their own "road blocks" into a "road trip" full of opportunities.

> "Pursue some path, however narrow and crooked, in which you can walk with love and reverence."
>
> ~Henry David Thoreau

You can read more about Celeste on her author page at amazon.com/author/celestecooper and about her role on Sharecare.com at http://www.sharecare.com/user/celeste-cooper. Check out her website at http://TheseThree.com for helpful patient information and links to her blog, social networks, and advocacy projects.

ABOUT THE AUTHOR, Jeff Miller, PhD

ॐ

Among other interests, Jeff values working with patients with chronic pain and illness. Through his expertise, he is able to help his clients cope with the many aspects of chronic illness. Jeff offers a variety of techniques including cognitive restructuring, biofeedback, hypnosis, and proactive utilization of gifts and skills from areas of strength adapted to areas of challenge.

His interest in chronic illness has become a sub-specialty, blending his pragmatic counseling with each individual's spiritual perspective. Jeff's goal for his life/work is to reduce suffering and help others live to their true potential. Jeff's mantra is *"If you want courage as your companion, do it now; do it even though you judge that courage insufficient because it is a diminishing thing, like water held in your palms. You will never be this brave again until the next time you face this. Then you will see (as you have seen) the smallest action is mightier than the noblest intention."*

His evolution from Lapsed Lutheran to Vajrayana Buddhist occurred in the early 1990s under the wary eye of mentors

Lama Surya Das, Shanti Mayi, Lama Chuck Sanford and a driver for Sedona Arizona's Pink Jeep Tours. Karmic forces deliver blows to the head by metaphoric 2X4s whenever he gets off topic.

Jeff is currently in his third decade of post-graduate education, having secured the enviable position of "paid student" by sitting in his comfortable office and awaiting his hourly lessons from folks who somehow believe he is there to help them. He is grateful above all for the trust of thousands of people in pain and for the nourishing unconditional love of his family. Jeff also gratefully acknowledges the guidance of many colleagues, especially his first boss who taught him which end of the horse he did not want to be.

Jeff is co-author with Celeste of *Integrative Therapies for Fibromyalgia, Chronic Fatigue Syndrome, and Myofascial Pain: The Mind-Body Connection.* Healing Arts Press: Vermont, 2010, and *Broken Body, Wounded Spirit: Balancing the SeeSaw of Chronic Pain* [Series], ImPress Media.

Coming soon: "*Stomping On Eggshells: the other side of psychotherapy.*"

Jeff's Website is *http://jeffmiller.org*

Other books written by Celeste Cooper and Jeff Miller
(Available in worldwide markets)

Broken Body, Wounded Spirit:
Balancing the SeeSaw of Chronic Pain,
SPRING DEVOTIONS

ImPress Media, Revised 2014.

Amazon in paperback
http://www.amazon.com/dp/0615958664/

Kindle version
http://www.amazon.com/dp/B00J1AOAR4

Amazon UK
http://www.amazon.co.uk/dp/0615958664/

Amazon Canada
http://www.amazon.ca/dp/0615958664/

Barnes and Nobel
http://www.barnesandnoble.com/w/1118934577?ean=9780615958668

Broken Body, Wounded Spirit:
Balancing the SeeSaw of Chronic Pain,
SUMMER DEVOTIONS

ImPress Media, Revised 2014.

ॐ

Amazon in paperback
www.amazon.com/dp/0615798268
Kindle version
www.amazon.com/dp/B00D665FPK
Amazon UK
www.amazon.co.uk/dp/0615798268
Amazon Canada
www.amazon.ca/dp/0615798268
Barnes and Nobel
www.barnesandnoble.com/w/1115477515?ean=9780615798264

ॐ

Broken Body, Wounded Spirit:
Balancing the SeeSaw of Chronic Pain,
WINTER DEVOTIONS

ImPress Media, Revised 2014.

ॐ

Amazon in paperback
http://www.amazon.com/dp/0615924050

Kindle version
http://www.amazon.com/dp/B00HAVXLYO/

Amazon UK
http://www.amazon.co.uk/dp/0615924050

Amazon Canada
http://www.amazon.ca//dp/0615924050

Barnes and Nobel
http://www.barnesandnoble.com/w/1118942182?ean=9780615924052

ॐ

Integrative Therapies for Fibromyalgia, Chronic Fatigue Syndrome, and Myofascial Pain: The Mind body Connection

Vermont: Healing Arts Press, 2010

Inner Traditions: Healing Arts Press (Publisher)
http://store.innertraditions.com/pages/browse

Amazon in paperback
www.amazon.com/dp/1594773238

Kindle version
www.amazon.com/dp/B003ZHVBAI

Amazon UK
www.amazon.co.uk/dp/1594773238

Amazon Canada.
www.amazon.ca/dp/1594773238

Barnes and Nobel
www.barnesandnoble.com/w/1112172406?ean=9781594773235

Nook Book
www.barnesandnoble.com/w/1112172406?ean=9781594779596

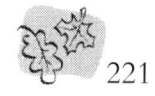

Made in the USA
Charleston, SC
01 October 2015